THE WASTE OF NATIONS

An Institute for Policy Studies Book

THE WASTE OF NATIONS
Dysfunction in the World Economy

DOUGLAS DOWD

WESTVIEW PRESS
BOULDER AND LONDON

An Institute for Policy Studies Book

Copyright © 1989 by Douglas Dowd

Published in 1989 in the United States of America by Westview Press, Inc., 5500 Central Avenue, Boulder, Colorado 80301, and in the United Kingdom by Westview Press, Inc., 13 Brunswick Centre, London WC1N 1AF, England

Library of Congress Cataloging-in-Publication Data
Dowd, Douglas Fitzgerald, 1919–
  The waste of nations / Douglas Dowd.
    p. cm.
"An Institute for Policy Studies book"—P.
  Bibliography: p.
  Includes index.
  ISBN 0-8133-0809-7. ISBN 0-8133-0810-0 (pbk.)
  1. Waste (Economics). 2. Economic policy. 3. Capitalism.
4. Waste (Economics)—United States. 5. United States—Economic
policy. 6. Capitalism—United States. I. Title.
HC79.W3D69   1989
338.9—dc19   88-26107
                                                                               CIP

Printed and bound in the United States of America

⊗   The paper used in this publication meets the requirements of the American National
     Standard for Permanence of Paper for Printed Library Materials Z39.48-1984.

10   9   8   7   6   5   4   3   2   1

For Anna

Contents

Preface

Not so long ago, the United States led a buoyant world economy in production, productivity, and lending; it leads still, but now in borrowing and spending, and in wasting. And today the world economy is beset by overcapacity, conflict, and nervousness. How can such a momentous reversal be explained?

It is tempting, even easy, to find the answer in wrong-headed leadership and misguided policy, especially that of the recent past in the United States. The leaders and their policy do bear some responsibility, but that can only be a part, and not the most important part, of an adequate explanation. We must also look elsewhere, to the tidal processes of capitalism, nationalism, and modern technology. The interaction of these started to set the direction and rhythms of the world at the beginning of the nineteenth century and when the industrial and social revolutions spread. In the twentieth century the mutually transforming impact of these economic, political, and technological forces has become even more fundamental. Only rarely have the quality of leadership and related policies been crucial in determining the main flows of the world economy, although they have often stimulated or retarded movements already under way. In general, a buoyant world economy makes leaders seem great, and a sagging world economy makes them appear to be fools. The ominous tendencies of today's economies cry out for far-reaching changes in economic and social policy, but as I will argue later, contemporary leadership is looking nostalgically to an imagined past for solutions.

This book will try to support the foregoing generalizations, as I explore the bases of capitalism and the world economy, past and present; but both the book's analysis and its intentions go beyond that. I believe the productive overcapacity and financial instability that characterize today's national and global economies threaten a major disaster in the very near future; I see the current situation as one of world economic crisis. The term crisis is used to suggest a historical turning point; my analysis and proposals for change assume that ordinary people need not and dare not remain passive observers concerning its resolution. A brief summary of the argument and proposed reforms are in order here.

For about twenty-five years after World War II, the dominant capitalist nations enjoyed a period of rapid and pervasive economic growth. The expansion of production, trade, income, and consumption, a quantitative movement, was made possible only by an underlying transformation of economic, political, and social institutions; that is, by a set of qualitative changes. Withal, the world economy began to slow down in the early 1970s. Since then, its hallmark has not been buoyancy but trouble—trouble with seriously rising prices, and especially the most important of them, the prices of money (interest rates) and oil; trouble with high levels of unemployment; trouble with debts and deficits; trouble with competition for global markets; all kinds of troubles and problems and associated doubts and worries, edging at times toward panic.

There is widespread agreement that what is now badly needed is a return to rapid rates of global economic expansion. But that *growth* cannot occur without a new stage of *development*: Another transformation of the structures of production, trade, and consumption is required and will be wrought only through institutional reforms. Few indeed have been the voices calling for the needed changes, and none at all from the mainstream of the social sciences, business, or government. This book, with its analytical and programmatic origins located at varying distances from the center, stands as another voice for substantial change. It differs from other off-center diagnoses and appeals, not so much in all of its warnings and programs, but in its emphasis upon waste as being critically responsible for much that goes badly in the world today and in its argument that the reduction of waste can serve as the principal means for beginning to resolve the present crisis in a beneficial manner.

Waste is a major characteristic of the contemporary political economy in the world, most particularly in the United States. The nature and the amounts of waste in this country are discussed at length in Chapter 4, as is the myopically limited definition of efficiency accepted by conventional economics, whose main practitioners put one in mind of "blind guides which strain at a gnat, and swallow a camel" (Matt., 23:24). They treat lightly, or more often not at all, the immense amounts of labor, capital equipment, and natural resources chronically wasted (in military and restricted agricultural and industrial production, planned product obsolescence, advertising and packaging, and so forth) and those left idle (cultivable acreage, closed factories and mines, and, most important of all, under- and unemployed labor).

A considerable amount of this waste is connected to complex strategies for maintaining profits by creating market scarcities. Meanwhile, most of the world's people, some in rich but the largest part by far in poor countries, suffer from terrible shortages of basic necessities and of capital equipment. To move from wasteful to useful practices in the world economy and to the higher levels of production, trade, and consumption thereby made possible, would require little change in the basic institutions of capitalism and nationalism, certainly not more than was required to bring forth the post–World War II buoyant world economy. But there is an important difference between then and now. It is that the earlier transformation of capitalism was engineered almost entirely from the top down, whereas the changes now needed must be effected largely by the political efforts and imagination of people from the middle and bottom layers of society.

Two serious criticisms may be readily anticipated: The analysis is too gloomy, and/or the program for change is too optimistic. I hope very much that the analysis is too gloomy, for if it is correct—and if the proposals are naively optimistic—we are in for a horrifying future. We have learned to take all predictions with a large grain of salt, as I do my own; but what I have forecast seems *so* likely and *so* dangerous that valor seemed the better part of discretion. As for the foolishness of thinking hopefully about reforms, and about people acting rationally in their own long-term interest, I think it is more foolish to sell people short, especially when they have any idea of what is going on. Thus, and only by way of example, few if any in the 1920s would have thought a New Deal possible in the United States a decade later (or nazism in Germany, and the pit into which it took the Germans); nor in the "silent 1950s" were there any who anticipated the turbulence of the 1960s. Neither the New Deal nor that turbulence resolved the problems it sought to treat, but both accomplished something worthwhile and lasting. And both taught us that there is more resilience in our species than appearances suggest (as the Nazi years warned us that there are depths below depths our species will plumb). I remain unshaken in my belief that where there's life, there's hope.

I first embarked on this book reluctantly, prodded toward it by the persistent questioning of Patricia Ellsberg. She wished to know if it was possible for capitalism to survive with less military production and less exploitation. I replied that it was possible, but that the offsetting changes required were entirely implausible. After some more prodding, I began to think seriously about the question instead of allowing habits of mind to supply the answers. That led to a draft for a long article, the criticisms of which by Daniel Ellsberg induced me to think and study even more; and the long article has become a not very long book. As a reading of the book will show, although I remain skeptical of possibility becoming probability, I also think there is a clear chance for it to happen.

The resulting book is, I think, useful for all seeking to understand contemporary capitalism, whether they are in or out of universities, whether in classes in economics, political science, or sociology, in environmental studies or history; and I hope it will be particularly useful for those working in groups dedicated politically to changing society toward peace, full employment, opened factories, clean air and water, equality of opportunity, and decent levels of health, education, and housing for all, everywhere. The message of this book is that there is no need for anyone in the world to live badly, and that it is downright dangerous to everyone that so many do so, that so many endure (and perish from) desperately poor lives.

It is a kind of arrogance to try to teach, in the classroom or a book; but as Willy Loman said in another connection, "It goes with the territory." I wish very much to thank those who encouraged me and helped me in that arrogance. First among them is Anna Hilbe, whose love and respect for life renewed my own and gave me energy when I most needed it. Before and since I began to write this book I have been much inspired and aided intellectually and politically by Jim O'Connor and Bruce Dancis, for many years *i miei veri compagni*. The editors of the Westview team, led by Barbara Ellington and Beverly LeSuer, have made what can be an irritating process into a pleasant one. I wish to add that in what has been a generally happy experience with editors from other publishers, the close work and critical comments of Marian Safran at Westview were the very best I have (happily) put up with. I thank her very much.

That the Institute for Policy Studies is participating in the publication of my book is most gratifying to me, for I have long seen it as a vital and constructive element in the efforts to redirect the social process of the United States. Saul Landau of the institute has been vitally helpful in important ways. Dr. Bertram Rosen of New York City and Professors Adrian Lyttelton and Stefano Zamagni of the Bologna Center of the School of Advanced International Studies of Johns Hopkins University have also assisted, and I thank them.

Doubtless, errors of omission and commission remain, but they have not been due to those who have tried to help me.

Douglas Dowd
San Francisco, California

CHAPTER 1

Threats and Opportunities of the Faltering World Economy

Introduction

Economic crisis has tossed and turned the world since the early 1970s, affecting every nation seriously, though in many and diverse ways. The pressures are lessened now and then, or here and there, but the crisis digs in always more deeply, as its scope steadily widens. In the absence of meaningful resolution, the world's economic problems tighten their grip, become more intractable, more menacing, and more disruptive of the entire social process. Those in business, government, and the universities, whose function it is to understand and to cope, have barely understood the world economic situation and have seen it not so much as a crisis as a series of unfortunate mishaps or temporary difficulties.[1]

Much of what can and should be done about the economy is obscured by ideology and received opinion; when pushed beyond that conventional wisdom one can see that this looming disaster is the result of processes that could be turned to the good. In fact, the means for averting tragedy could also create a safer, saner, and better world.

Such optimistic phrases are not idle dreams. Although there is too much productive capacity in agriculture and industry worldwide to sustain general profitability and full employment, for most of the world's people there is far too little of what is needed to sustain life decently or—for many millions each year—at all. And set between these problems of too much and too little there are immense mountains of waste: in what *is* produced (a large part of it military waste) and in what could be, but *is not*, produced (that is, unutilized productive capacities in agriculture and industry, and underutilized or nonutilized labor). For the United States, for example, the facts are mind-boggling: As will be discussed at length in Chapter 4, it is probably an understatement to identify about half of U.S. production as wasteful, as serving no useful purpose—and this ignores the amounts of nonproduction.

Good sense and imagination, considerable political effort, and a less ideological approach can, indeed must, devise and implement policies that would simultaneously level the mountains of waste and use the released productive capacities to raise the material well-being of the world's people. That such a transformation would be politically difficult goes without saying. But because it is *economically* realistic within the main institutions of the status quo (capitalism and nationalism), it is therefore more than a pipe dream.

It will be argued throughout this book that the ends and means of this path to a better world are both practical and appealing to a broad range of people and groups in all nations. It can happen. And if it does not? Then the now-chronic world economic crisis will continue to take society toward economic and quite possibly military catastrophe. Skepticism is both necessary and widespread in this world, but it is worth noting that along with the decade's ugly and shocking developments, the 1980s have also produced some hopeful surprises, not the least of which has been the measured movement toward arms control between the Soviet Union and the United States. Arms control as such does not imply reductions in military production, but it is a first step in the appropriate direction. And who would have thought it possible, let us say, in the mid-1980s?

That first step in arms control became possible in critical part because it is a sine qua non of Mikhail Gorbachev's policy of *perestroika*. The term means restructuring, and there can be no structural changes in the Soviet economy without a considerable reduction in military spending. That the economy of the United States needs structural changes also has been clear for some years: There is no other way to bring the national and foreign debt under control. In both countries, such economic transformations would require a changing mentality. If, as, and when the United States (and the Soviet Union) takes the lead in making structural changes, it will become easier and necessary for the other nations of the world, rich and poor, to find their own ways to change for the better.

There have long been strong arguments for eliminating worldwide waste, both military and nonmilitary. Such arguments have taken on a compelling force in the late 1980s because of the world economic crisis and because that crisis, although earlier slowed and deflected by the practices, the jobs, and the profits of waste, has been exacerbated by the costs, the economic drag, the negative consequences of wasteful production and nonproduction (as will be shown in later chapters).

Crisis tendencies became evident for the first time in 1971, after the longest, broadest, and most substantial period of economic expansion in capitalist (or any other) history. The expansion that took hold as the 1950s began far overshadowed in every way the British-led expansion of the nineteenth century, for example, or that of the United States in the 1920s.[2]

The pervasive buoyancy of the world economy and its member nations in the post–World War II era was both the result of and the continuing basis for a complex and interdependent set of institutional changes within and outside the United States, largely put together and dominated by the United States. The alterations were simultaneously economic and political, military and cultural, overlapping and mutually reinforcing, in what emerged as a tightly integrated world economy. Altogether, the institutional changes constituted a new stage of capitalist development, and it was a necessary new stage, if capitalism was to come back to life after the bloody and devastating decades that culminated in World War II.

The changes began at Bretton Woods (New Hampshire) in 1944, when the International Monetary Fund (IMF) and the World Bank were born. The many later steps included the General Agreement on Tariffs and Trade (GATT), the Marshall Plan, the North Atlantic Treaty Organization (NATO), and in 1957, the Treaty of Rome (establishing the European Common Market). The last named was made possible by the agreements that preceded it; it paved the way for further cooperation.

Also beginning with the end of World War II, Japan's economy was placed under U.S. supervision. Remaining highly concentrated and centralized in its political economy, Japan was much invigorated by the reforms instituted and perhaps even more so by the economic side effects of U.S. foreign and military policies and activities toward China, Korea, and Indochina.

Moreover, the prewar structure of imperialist power was transformed, giving the United States a position of economic privilege and political, military, and cultural influence exceeding that held earlier by all other nations in the world put together. "The American Century" touted by Henry Luce and his influential journals (*Time*, *Life*, and *Fortune* among them) in the years surrounding World War II had begun. Although it is unlikely to last a century, it has at least endured longer than the "Thousand Year Reich."[3]

Within that overall process of change, the growing strength of the leading economies was nurtured by the modernized national capitalist state, which, in different ways in different countries, placed government in a position of "constructive guidance." In the United States more than elsewhere, this was accomplished by a symbiotic relationship between heavy "warfare and welfare" spending, joined to great increases in consumption, domestic and foreign investment, and world trade. Without the heavy military spending, all this was reproduced in the other major Western powers.

Each of the foregoing both made possible and depended upon the other changes (and more yet to be noted); all required an ever-deeper penetration of the neocolonial, that is, politically independent, but economically dependent, societies. In response to the carrots and sticks of the awesome economic and military strength of the United States after World War II, Americanization—or, as President de Gaulle was reputed to have said, "Coca-colonization"—spread over the globe, including a good part of the noncapitalist world. But after less than twenty years of this striking accomplishment, the very institutions and processes that had made for the successes of the new capitalist system began slowly but surely to create conflicts, strains, and problems.

The oil shocks of 1973 and subsequently are universally seen as the real cause of the economic troubles that mark the path to the problems of the 1980s. But this requires succumbing to the historical amnesia that has become so common. The first serious signs of systemic deterioration occurred well before the Organization of Petroleum Exporting Countries (OPEC) oil price increases initiated in December 1973.

As David Calleo pointed out,

By August 1971, with domestic inflation again rising and the dollar clearly heading for a fall, Nixon was ready with his political masterstroke, the "New Economic Policy." On August 15, with the currency markets in crisis, Nixon himself announced the new policy. The measures amounted to a sort of mercantilist revolution in domestic and foreign policy. The dollar's official convertibility into either gold or foreign currencies was suspended indefinitely, and a temporary surcharge of 10% was imposed on dutiable imports. At home, wages, prices, and rents were frozen for ninety days, while both federal taxes and expenditures were cut.[4]

And in 1973, the fixed exchange rate system was abandoned.

Not only did this new economic policy (NEP) (one cannot help but wonder if Nixon knew of Lenin's NEP) repudiate global economic arrangements put together by the United States from the time of Bretton Woods on, it also signified that the world's most recent emperor was unable to learn to speak his lines properly.

Also occurring before 1973, adding fuel to the fire, and arising from the main policies that had worked to create bustling national and international economic activity, what came to be called "stagflation"—the continuing tendency of national economies simultaneously to generate persisting inflation along with persisting unemployment—made its historical debut. Stagflation is a combination of processes defying all the precepts of conventional economic theory and is made all the more vicious in practice because the attempt to alleviate one problem promptly exacerbates the other.[5]

The extraordinary oil price increases of and after the winter of 1973–1974 of course made a bad situation considerably worse, further weakening an already shaky set of structures. But those price increases were themselves a defensive response by OPEC countries to a serious inflation already well under way: Between 1970 and 1973, in the leading capitalist countries, the rates of price increases were generally at least three times such rates in the 1960s, in some cases going into double digits. Furthermore, that OPEC *could* take such an aggressive action was in itself a clear sign of a major crack in the postwar institutional structure and of the growing inability of the major powers to have their way in the Third World, whether Indochina, southern Africa, Central America, or the Middle East.[6]

Capitalist political economy works well in its own terms only when there is a dynamic and integrated world economy (as will be elaborated upon in Chapter 3). The latter in turn depends upon the major national economies' acceptance of their participation in the global system as both essential and beneficial for them. But such voluntary acquiescence can and will occur only when economic expansion is pervasive, strong, and expected to continue.

These conditions could not all be met as the 1970s began. The continuing breakdown of the international monetary and trade systems and the onset of stagflation forced nations to seek ways to protect themselves. The lead was taken not by the weakest but by the strongest, the hegemonic nation, the United States. The results ate away at the foundations of an integrated world economy and thus rendered more difficult the functioning of both global and national economic activities.

Soon both the politics and the economics of redesigned capitalism—which I shall discuss as "monopoly capitalism"—began to erode the achievements of the system and to place under serious questioning the very policies that had made it work smoothly. Most important of these national developments had been the ones that depended upon a congenial and mutually "permissive" set of relationships between what in the United States are called big business, big labor, and big government. Critical among such policies[7] were those that markedly raised levels of real consumption and investment, stimulated world trade, and improved both economic and political stability (benefiting the bottom four-fifths of the population in the leading nations as well as, even more, those in the top fifth). All this was aided and abetted by an unprecedentedly pervasive and profitable movement into the socioeconomic life of the neocolonial world.

Backward into the Future

In later chapters the origins and principles of both early ("competitive") and contemporary ("monopoly") capitalism will be defined, discussed, and analyzed in their national and global features, and I shall examine their structures and processes, their waxing and waning. Suffice it to say here that as the present system has been losing its dynamism, quite conservative and/or reactionary governments in virtually all of the powerful capitalist nations have come to power, along with a substantial revival of the ideology and some of the practices of competitive capitalism. This reaching back into the past for economic solutions, a reaction to the long years of crisis, increases the probability that a chronic and already serious world economic slowdown will degenerate into a tragedy of horrifying dimensions.

This devolution seems especially likely when one considers that in the brief span of years since 1980, the world system's dominant power—the United States—has been transformed from the world's leading creditor to its leading debtor nation (its foreign debt expected to reach $1 trillion by 1992). The United States has also discovered the most substantial part of its external creditor position to be more of a threat than an advantage; it has seen its industrial base gutted and its major businesses turn to financial roulette and, as one economist recently put it, become best "at going out of business." The United States has fecklessly doubled its national public debt (to well over $2 trillion), as its consumer and business debt has also surpassed dangerous levels ("dangerous" because neither the public nor the private debt has been sufficiently used for productive purposes and because of the methods of acquiring both kinds of debt, not because of the levels as such). The nation has become ever more reckless in both its military expenditures and its associated activities, whether open or covert, and has had its political leadership revealed as alarmingly corrupt even by historically low standards and system-atically deceptive and self-destructive: its military "successes" measured by the Grenada escapade, its economic "successes" measured by a wrenching recession to reduce inflation, followed by an economic ex-pansion made possible solely by record-breaking budget deficits whose causes and consequences are not only denied but probably not even comprehended by their creator.

When one considers that the only nation if any that might be able to lead the world economy out of crisis has done quite the opposite and that its main policy goals amount to attempts to recreate some mixture of the political economy of Calvin Coolidge and the foreign policy of Teddy Roosevelt (in a society whose upper levels mimic the decadence and immature behavior of the 1920s), then it would also seem necessary to search seriously for ways and means and goals that go well beyond the conventional wisdom of this century.

The nostalgic fantasies and ruthless actions of the Reagans and Thatchers have heightened the incomes and wealth of those at the top, but at the same time and for the same reasons these fantasies and actions succeeded in worsening rather than alleviating the entrenched crisis.[8] But not much more can be said for current programs that have "liberal" or "Keynesian" components (as those terms are presently understood), stemming from the belief that the techniques and policies of state management developed after World War II remain sufficient for resolving today's difficulties. Such an approach sees problems as quantitative (the dollar is too strong) or cyclical (macroeconomic) in nature. But today's problems are structural, institutional, and qualitative. They are in many ways an outcome of the very "corporate liberal" policies that are still believed in—except by those in power who yearn for the simplicities of an idealized, distant, and brutal past. In short, what in the late 1980s seem to be ugly flowers are those that, in their earlier days, were thought beauteous; they are, in any case, flowers from the same plant. The policies that once were functional have become dysfunctional because of the ways in which they succeeded—the only ways, under capitalism, they could succeed. Why that is so will be explored in the pages to come.

The new and modified structures and processes that came into being after World War II regenerated world capitalism; but in doing so they brought into being a system that as time has gone on has made those same structures and processes "old": Military Keynesianism, tax reforms (and their upward redistributions of income and wealth), and frequent attempts to manipulate exchange rates and trade balances, when they have worked, have also, like many modern medications, had deleterious side effects (as will be discussed further in Chapters 2 and 3).

Far from diminishing global instability and economic deterioration, present policies have deepened the problems of national and world economy, postponing the day of reckoning, but at the price of increasing and spreading the costs for the economy. For example, the supply-side economics and tax reforms of the Reagan years were sold to the public as nostrums for increasing productive capacity and productivity and, via increased real incomes and jobs, tax collections. But it was takeovers and financial speculation, considerably more than real investment, that grew in the following years. Alternatively, as Mexico and other Latin American countries fell into de facto default on their North American loans after 1982, it was "restructuring" that was hailed as a solution. The years following have seen such restructuring revealed as a way of disguising the hopeless economic conditions of the debtors and the reckless management practices of the creditors, whose numbers include most of the top banks in the United States. As a final example, I can point to the managed decline of the dollar after late 1985. Despite a fall in the dollar's value against major currencies of anywhere from 40 to 50 percent, the U.S. trade deficit in 1986 exceeded the deficits of 1984 and 1985, and that of 1987 broke all records. Exports rose significantly in 1988, but so too did imports; and the foreign debt moves inexorably to the $1 trillion mark. (It is estimated that more than two million industrial jobs have been lost in the United States as that debt has risen.[9])

At the heart of the long-standing crisis is an insoluble dilemma: What appear to be solutions to one problem, such as the Third World debt or the U.S. trade deficit, turn out to be causes of another problem, even more severe. For example, solutions to the Third World debt make Third World countries unable to maintain imports (or even political stability); solutions to the U.S. trade deficit cause worldwide recession because falling U.S. imports mean falling world exports.

What then are the structures and the institutions, the qualitative characteristics that underly and have brought the world to this state of affairs? What is it that receives too little, or no, attention from the mainstream economists and politicians of the center and right?

Accumulate, Waste, and Want Not

A world economic crisis is of course a tangled process with complex origins. But it has an economic center. The crisis of the present, like that which grew in the 1920s, finds its center in the existence of pervasive and growing excess capacity: in all sectors of the economy and in all parts of the capitalist world economy. This overcapacity is the unavoidable outcome of several characteristics intrinsic to the capitalist process, whether that of the nineteenth or of this century: (1) investment and production both in principle and in practice taking place without national or international planning; (2) businesses and nations, to survive and to flourish in the ruthless struggle for profits and power, participating in the latest technologies in the leading industries of their epoch and thus constantly increasing production and productivity. So far so good; indeed these two characteristics in action provide the largest part of the ideological support for the system. But there is another feature intrinsic to the capitalist process: (3) its highly unequal distribution of income (and of wealth and power, which maintain or make more unequal the distribution of income). Essential for allowing the vital process of capital accumulation and its profitability, this inequity also sets limits on the system's capacity for absorbing its own production, providing it with the need to expand continuously through more debt and more investment (thus adding to productive capacity and productivity even more) as well as geographically (seeking new markets, privileged access to raw materials, cheap labor, investment outlets, strategic locations). The ultimate consequences have included: (4) duplicative, redundant, excess global productive capacities. In their beginnings these developments, in one way or another, were encouraged by the capitalist state; as the dog days arrived, the state, in one way or another, sought to protect the affected industries from competitive evil doers.

The twentieth century has witnessed a profound increase in the ability to transform and expand production. In its first decades, the inability of businesses and governments to control rising excess capacities contributed decisively to the chaos, convulsions, wars, economic catastrophes, and political upheavals that assaulted the entire world after 1914. At least a few of those who were or who became economically and politically influential after those terrible years learned something from all the disorder and violence and the threats to the very survival of capitalism. Among those few was John Maynard Keynes. But what he learned and taught in his writings was interpreted narrowly and applied at its most callous level; had that not been so, it is quite unlikely that President Richard Nixon would have made his famous remark: "We are all Keynesians now." Keynes, like his great predecessors who sought to build and guide the capitalist system—Adam Smith and David Ricardo and John Stuart Mill—would have scorned his inheritors, the "macro-economists," for what they have utilized from his works and how they have done it, and castigated them for what they have ignored.[10]

Since World War II there has developed a more or less coherent, self-conscious, and until recently, effective confrontation of the problem of great and growing productive capacity in the capitalist world economy. The solution is *waste*. The waste is systematic and institutionalized, as measured by what is produced and how and by what is withheld from use and/or is destroyed. This broad pattern of waste is accompanied by messages from business and government that seek to dignify waste with other names: national security, or fashion, or preserving the family farm, or safety, or freedom, or efficiency, or . . . The messages are essential, given the deep-seated tradition (not least in the United States) of Ben Franklin's "waste nothing."

Facilitating the long expansion after World War II, and in turn made possible by it, was an immense, always increasing, and by the late 1980s incredible, amount of withheld and wasted production, including, but by no means confined to, stupefying levels of military spending throughout the world: over $1 trillion a year. In this, as in so much else, the leader is the United States. It has also taken the lead in the frequent and destructive *uses* of military products in Asia, Latin America, the Middle East, and Africa.[11] In Chapter 4 the political economy of waste will be examined at length. There we shall see that in addition to about half of all production that is wasted one must add a considerable amount that could be but is not produced—from unused or underutilized labor, land, and equipment. All this has occurred at a time and in a world incessantly setting off alarms about scarcity.

The waste of productive capacity, of human energy and skills, and of almost all natural resources must be seen as systemic, as a principal way in which the system survives, in both peace and war. It has served the vital purposes of helping to postpone or soften economic crises, of keeping the social peace at home, and of maintaining the structures of profit and power over the globe. As such, it is not waste for the system; for humanity, it is terrible waste and much more.

Could such a pervasive development have occurred without a conscious and coordinated decision to that end? It seems so, and not only because there is no evidence of a conscious conspiracy to bring it about. As many small streams finally converge to make a river, so it was with the historical process that now floods economies with waste. The processes of waste began years before they became critical to the system, long before they came together to assist in the survival of capitalism.

Given the strong tendencies toward excess and unprofitable productive capacity in this century, there seemed to be only two general alternatives: either socialism, which would eliminate capitalism along with its over-capacities, or fascism—which, acceptable as it was to those in power in several nations (Italy, Germany, and Japan, among the most powerful), showed itself to be a vicious and piratical form of capitalism. Knowing that the United States would be the sole vigorous survivor of that tortured half century, one may say that it was a virtual certainty that neither the socialist nor the fascist path would, finally, be found acceptable.[12] Waste, if effectively camouflaged, could serve as a satisfactory alternative.

If a formative period had to be identified, it would be the decade 1915–1925. In those years two major developments entered the consciousness and lives of people in business and government in the United States, on its "boyish" way to becoming the most powerful nation in the world's history: (1) the economic and social-political meaning of war and patriotism; (2) the decision in what was already the dominant industry in the United States, automobile manufacturing, to introduce simultaneously the annual model change, advertising, and consumer

on was first put into effect by General Motors in
se innovations soon spread into the consumer durable
wherever feasible.
to transpire before patriotic and business waste could
lized, become accepted as the air one breathes (whether
d), seen as normal, natural, and right. Both the military
were unpopular in the United States in the 1930s, but
nged by World War II. Between them, the depression
e maturation of the advertising profession for selling
ideas, the popularity of World War II economically and
e good war"), and the implantation of the cold war
is not only anti-Communist but also procapitalist) meant
ely sophisticated and informed business and political
nerged after the war would rather easily find themselves
social order, one depending upon extraordinary waste.
er the past decade or so, when these elements were put
others making for trouble in the global capitalist system,
of waste, most especially those in the military realm,
worsen than to relieve the persisting crisis. In the United
ncome levels for all but a small percentage have stabilized
ce the 1970s,[13] it has become easier to see the linkages
ve military spending and massive budget deficits, decline
fficiency on the one hand and rising trade deficits and
the other, and how all these are related to the loss of
manageability of the U.S. and world economy. Obviously
elements involved in that chain, but military waste holds
her and in place. In my concluding chapter I will argue
pally this massive waste that makes it possible to move
saner, and more decent world. For of course it is true
rich part of the world is wasting so much, billions of
rately little. The bridge between those two socioeconomic worlds can be constructed by transforming waste into useful
production.

Is There a Road from Here to There?

In the absence of substantial change in institutions and in attitudes
toward what is desirable, necessary, and possible, there is no reason to
expect the current crisis to be resolved acceptably, that is, by significant
worldwide economic expansion at real growth rates well in excess of
those at present or foreseen. Instead, the probabilities narrow down to
two: Either the crisis will become much more of a disaster (it is already
a disaster to a large percentage of the world's people), with unknowable

but terrible prospects,[14] or to forestall that, capitalist institutions must be changed once more, at least as much as they were in the 1950s and 1960s, in some similar and in some different directions. Those institutions must be changed to alter structures of production, consumption, world trade, and investment and to broaden the access to policymaking as well. They must be changed in the direction of "de-wastification" (not least through reduced military production) and further democratization, both nationally and globally, changed so as to use, rather than to waste and destroy precious productive capacities. The waste of this human potential, when people are underemployed or unemployed, is the worst consequence of the chain of events beginning with massive military spending, which leads to massive budget deficits, decline in productive efficiency, rising trade deficits, and rising foreign debt.

Some may envision an attractive third possibility, namely, the rapid and beneficial spread of democratic socialism in the world. But, as will be noted later, one of the consequences of capitalism's recent history has been the demoralization and weakening of the forces that might hasten such a development throughout the capitalist world and the effective hobbling and distortion of socialism, through one form or another of intervention, in the countries where it has emerged. Perhaps the most steadily effective impediment to the spread of democratic socialism has been the need for the socialist countries to militarize their economies, thus intensifying other weaknesses—probably a conscious aim of U.S. policy in the cold war.

The required changes within the basic capitalist framework of private ownership and production for profit to be proposed in Chapter 5 would most probably be resisted or scorned (if for different reasons) by those on the left, the middle, and the right—the Left skeptical of benign changes and in any case reluctant to prolong capitalism's life span; the Middle hoping to muddle through to a light at the end of the tunnel; and the Right once more preferring to save the system by variations on fascism. In the critical decade after 1945, all three of these political clusters would quite probably have scorned the totality of changes that in fact began to emerge (but that as a totality were never "proposed"); and especially for those of the Left, with good reason. Speaking, however, to those still somewhere on the left (myself included), one may hope that growing awareness of the combination of threats, needs, and possibilities contained in the crisis of the late 1980s, along with the enfeebled condition of the Left, will help to alter judgments as to what constitutes constructive political behavior—before, rather than after, an unspeakable disaster. That this book is by no means the first to move along such lines indicates that this is not a vain hope.[15]

It will become the principal argument in what follows that the constructive and substantial reduction of wasted and withheld production is at one and the same time the only way to slow down and to reverse the trends of the late 1980s toward economic and quite probably military tragedy of unprecedented proportions. What is more, it is seemingly the most promising basis upon which real progress could be made at this time toward both a more peaceful and a more equitable world.

Put differently, it is both necessary and possible to lift the levels of consumption of the bottom four-fifths of the world's people (without having to lower the incomes of the top fifth), thereby utilizing while altering existing and rising levels of productive capacity in agriculture, industry, and services over the entire globe. All of this can be financed by greatly reducing military (but not governmental) spending and converting the relevant productive facilities, while also transforming other areas of great waste (such as restricted agricultural and industrial production) in the world economy and assisting in the further economic development of countries whose productive capacities are far too low. Such changes would mean many things: Among the most important would be lowered levels of labor exploitation (a rough measure of which is increased real consumption) and reduction of international tension.[16]

Such proposals are unrealistic—of course. All proposals for changing a status quo are unrealistic and always have been. But are these more unrealistic than the dreams that see the crisis of the 1980s somehow fading away, to be replaced, somehow, by renewed expansion and increased real incomes for ordinary people, along with, somehow, a lessened threat of conventional and nuclear war? What C. Wright Mills called the "crackpot realism"[17] of those who preside over and acquiesce in the main tendencies of modern society is no less crazy for being widely accepted, no less crazy, either, than the leadership of the violent and destructive years before and after 1914. Certainly it is recognized that such leadership and such "realism" today are considerably more dangerous than ever before: We cannot bear another major depression; we cannot survive another major—that is, nuclear—war.

Socioeconomic analysis and proposals are something like medical diagnoses and prescription (and not only in the fallibility of both). Just as a doctor prescribing a serious operation should acquaint the patient with something of anatomy and physiology in general and in relevant particulars, it is necessary here, in order to find support for the proposals that conclude this book, to sketch the main structures and processes of this socioeconomic system, the conditions under which they work well and those within which they now work so tenuously, produce crisis, and thus require "a serious operation."

Mainstream economic and political commentators do not see the recent past and present as one of protracted crisis; nor did their counterparts in the 1920s. Irving Fisher pronounced in 1928 (when U.S. industrial production was already shaky, unemployment at disturbing levels, and the world economy in a shambles for many years), "We have solved the problem of the business cycle: the economy is on a high and rising plateau."[18] Though many of today's "experts" have begun to show signs of disquiet with the U.S. and the world economy, they point to short-run and aggregative, rather than long-run and structural, problems, to recent events rather than to tendencies, to current political leadership as a cause (when it is even more a consequence) of bothersome realities.[19]

I shall try to show instead that what has roiled the waters of the national and world economies since the 1970s is deep-seated, structural, and cumulatively destabilizing. The resulting crisis, one may hope, is unlikely to erupt momentarily; in the period in which, like an underwater volcano, it continues to sound its warnings, there may be time to initiate and to develop changes that, in slowly and steadily altering key economic and political structures and processes, can give us a changed direction, a different rhythm, some breathing space in which to avert disaster—even, perhaps, to create an atmosphere in which something more than disaster averted could be hoped for.

Thus, Chapter 2 will examine the ideology, the imperatives, and the always-changing realities of capitalism. More to the point, it will analyze the main institutions, structures, and processes of contemporary capitalism as they have emerged and grown and now decay. Chapter 3 will describe and analyze the critical role of the world economy in the functioning of capitalism, past and present, and the tendencies that now hasten its disintegration and malfunctioning. Chapter 4 will focus upon the political economy of waste and destruction, which, having done so much to allow and to cause social tragedy and to keep the system from sinking, must be turned to beneficial purposes, even though among those benefiting will most certainly be those who are responsible for the system's harmful policies—such is the way of the world. Finally, Chapter 5 will turn to the thesis of this book and summarily propose ways and means in the economy and in politics for the conversion of the waste-dependent and disaster-prone patterns of production to other patterns that could instead do as much to nourish life as now is done to damage it.[20]

Notes

1. "Barely understood," that is, by mainstream economists, with very few exceptions. One such exception is represented by Susan Strange and Roger Tooze (eds.), *The International Politics of Surplus Capacity* (London: Allen &

Unwin, 1981). Even in this very useful book, concerned with the 1970s, the depth of the crisis was not seen. See its Chapter 2, "Interpreting Excess Capacity." Radical economists have been busy for many years analyzing the onset and nature of this crisis, and references to their works will be made throughout the following pages. James O'Connor was among the first to perceive the cracks in the structure of contemporary capitalism in his *Fiscal Crisis of the State* (New York: St. Martin's Press, 1973) and more recently, in his *Accumulation Crisis* (New York: Blackwell, 1984). Harry Magdoff and Paul Sweezy, editors of *Monthly Review*, have written a continuing stream of essays exploring the crisis, now collected into four separate books: *The End of Prosperity* (1977), *The Dynamics of U.S. Capitalism* (1979), *The Deepening Crisis of U.S. Capitalism* (1980), and *Stagnation and the Financial Explosion* (1987) (New York: Monthly Review Press, years indicated).

2. Joseph A. Schumpeter, *Business Cycles: A Theoretical, Historical, and Statistical Analysis of the Capitalist Process*, 2 vols. (New York: McGraw-Hill, 1939), provided an astute and thorough survey; Robert A. Gordon, *Economic Instability and Growth: the American Record* (New York: Harper and Row, 1974), examined the years since 1919 in the United States.

3. The literature on these developments is of course immense. Among the most acute are Gabriel Kolko, *Main Currents in American History* (New York: Pantheon Books, 1984), especially pp. 310ff., Fred Block, *The Origins of International Economic Disorder* (Berkeley and London: University of California Press, 1977), and Walter Russell Mead, *Mortal Splendor: The American Empire in Transition* (Boston: Houghton Mifflin, 1987). Part 1 of Mead is a useful summary and analysis of the early years of the process. For a powerful critique and history of the expansion of U.S. power into (especially) Asia, see Noam Chomsky, *American Power and the New Mandarins* (New York: Pantheon Books, 1969), and more broadly, Harry Magdoff, *The Age of Imperialism: The Economics of U.S. Foreign Policy* (New York: Monthly Review Press, 1969).

4. David P. Calleo, *The Imperious Economy* (Cambridge, Mass.: Harvard University Press, 1982), pp. 62–63. Written from a liberal perspective, this book chronicled the rise and fall of the "Pax Americana" (in Calleo's terms) from the 1960s into the 1980s.

5. Stagflation will be discussed further in Chapter 2. I sought to explain its emergence and meanings in "Stagflation and the Political Economy of Decadent Monopoly Capitalism," *Monthly Review*, October 1976, and in *Rivista Internazionale di Scienze Economiche e Commerciale*, n. 10–11, 1976.

6. For oil and OPEC, see Michael Tanzer, *The Energy Crisis: World Struggle for Power and Wealth* (New York: Monthly Review Press, 1974); for the emergence of rising instability in the imperialist world, see Kolko, *Main Currents*, Chapters 10 and 11, and Yann Fitt, Alexandre Faire, and Jean-Pierre Vigier, *The World Economic Crisis* (London: Zed Press, 1976), which has many useful statistical tables, as well as a comprehensive analysis.

7. The reference here is to complex social expenditure programs, along with acquiescence in trade union demands that set floors to wages and ceilings to unemployment, while also allowing the growth of fringe benefits—most im-

portantly, those having to do with health and retirement. Altogether, these amounted to a lowering of the level of exploitation in the major countries, relatively painless to capital as long as the overall rate of economic expansion and profitability continued. That the "welfare" side of the welfare-warfare state began to be politically unpopular in the 1970s was the result of a new mixture of some old and some new tendencies in the United States (and to a lesser extent elsewhere), namely, the decline in real income and rise in unemployment as stagflation hardened and led the main elements of the industrial working class to listen to those who put the blame on high taxes and "wasteful social expenditures" benefiting (it was said) the mostly black poor. This trend strengthened an already rising tide of racism, not least as consumerist hopes were frustrated. The warfare side was of course given a supportive treatment and portrayed along with free-market arguments as being responsible for whatever well-being existed and continued. For an analysis that shows quite exactly that "the black poor" were more the victims than the beneficiaries of the politics and policies of the so-called welfare state, see William Julius Wilson, *The Truly Disadvantaged: The Inner City, the Underclass, and Public Policy* (Chicago: University of Chicago Press, 1987). Regarding militarization of the economy, see "Special Issue on Militarism," *Economic Forum,* Summer 1982. Among other articles in that issue is James Cypher's on "military Keynesianism," to be discussed later, and one by myself, "Militarized Economy, Brutalized Society."

8. Lester Thurow, in an important essay in *Scientific American,* May 1987, "A Surge in Inequality," showed how the shares of income and wealth of the highest layers have risen while those of the lowest and lower-middle layers have fallen. He explained the changes in terms of the functioning of the world economy and the "feminization of poverty" and saw improvement only through improved education and economic growth.

9. The woefully inadequate nature of steps taken and proposed can be understood from a reading of Stephen Marris, *Dollars and Deficits* (Washington, D.C.: International Economic Institute, 1985). That the reduction of the dollar's value of 40 to 50 percent since late 1985 has increased U.S. exports, finally, is of course true, but the strengthening of U.S. industry (especially its manufacturing sector) in the current process portends ill for the rest of the world in the absence of worldwide economic expansion—which nobody expects. See *Deficits and the Dollar Revisited: August 1987,* an update by Stephen Marris of the 1985 book (same publisher, 1987). Here Marris produced data that very closely confirm his gloomy expectations of 1985. After the restructuring of debt came to be seen as inadequate, Citicorp, followed by dozens of other banks, in effect wrote off large amounts of its loans by making additions to its "loan loss reserves." This was hailed at the time as both a sensible and a useful step. But just a year later, the *Wall Street Journal* featured a story whose headline reflected the pessimism that continues to surround the whole problem. See "Since '87 Loss Reserves, Latin Debt Crisis Has Grown: In a Vicious Circle, Bank Loans Dwindle—and So Might Payments," May 19, 1988.

10. In his *General Theory of Employment, Interest, and Money* (New York: Harcourt, Brace, 1937), and especially in his Chapter 12 on long-term investment,

in some lengthy footnotes, and in later essays, John Maynard Keynes argued that the chronic inadequacies of private effective demand (consumer plus investment expenditures) required continuous, large, and increasing amounts of what he termed "social consumption and investment." He also noted wryly that the demand gap could be filled by military expenditures ("building dreadnoughts and sinking them in the Atlantic Ocean") or by even more obvious waste ("setting some men to dig holes and others to fill them up"). Ominously, the first national economic program to apply Keynesian principles consciously (though not as Keynes would have, of course) was that of Finance Minister Hjalmar Schacht, in Nazi Germany. That program took Germany to full employment by 1938, while real per capita consumption declined.

11. See R. L. Sivard, *World Military and Social Expenditures* (Washington, D.C.: World Priorities, 1983), and Saadet Deger, *Military Expenditures in Third World Countries* (London: Routledge and Kegan Paul, 1986). In Chapter 4 I will discuss waste in detail and systematically.

12. Socialist possibilities were much vitiated in the United States in the years following World War I, for reasons internal and external to the movement, which had earlier grown to substantial strength. See James Weinstein, *Decline of Socialism* (New York: Random House, 1969). The depression of the 1930s brought a revival of but also increased the factionalism of the U.S. Left; and the cold war after 1945 dealt socialism an almost mortal blow. As for fascism: It is a response not only to crisis but also to a revolutionary threat. Except in feverish imaginations, there has been no such threat in the United States, whether prewar or postwar. Fascism also requires a level of sustained and widespread political seriousness, however grotesque, that has hitherto been lacking in the United States. That there are possibilities for a particularly American version of fascism, however, is discussed and analyzed well in Bertram Gross, *Friendly Fascism: The New Face of Power in America* (New York: M. Evans, 1980).

13. The statistics on income can be and usually are confusing and contradictory; they must be examined with great care. Thus: Real average earnings in the United States in 1986 were no higher than in 1962, but real income per head rose by 38 percent between 1960 and 1986 (in constant dollars). Solving the puzzle merely requires breaking the statistics down. "Real average earnings" excludes salary earners and covers only "production and non-supervisory workers." That is, "the gap between salary-earners and those below them has widened in real terms." For these and connected matters, see the *Economist* (Great Britain), October 31, 1987, p. 41. A more general and penetrating analysis is that of Frank Levy, *Dollars and Dreams: The Changing American Income Distribution* (New York: Basic Books, 1987). Levy showed the movement toward increased inequality from the mid-1960s to the mid-1980s, seeing the period between 1973 and 1984 for most of the people as one of "quiet depression." What Levy said of the people at the bottom in the United States must be repeated with much greater emphasis for the majority of people in the world, those in Africa, Asia, Latin America, and the Middle East. For perhaps three billion people, everyday life has become a "quiet disaster."

14. Although such a catastrophe might be initiated by economic breakdown (itself an outcome of larger social weaknesses) it could not fail to have alarming

social and political consequences, including a much enhanced possibility of global nuclear war. One cannot afford to forget the central role of economic collapse in the interwar period in producing the martial outcome of the 1930s. The world is at least as unstable in the late 1980s as it was then.

15. One should remember that the political efforts of organized labor and the Left, directed toward socialism, turned out to have been a major propelling force for, and responsible for much of the formulation of, socioeconomic reform of capitalism in the twentieth century. That input is likely to be both necessary and true for the future, if there are to be substantial and desirable changes, such as those proposed here.

16. Mead, *Mortal Splendor,* for somewhat different reasons and in different words, moved along this same path. See his Part 6.

17. See C. Wright Mills, *The Causes of World War Three* (New York: Ballantine Books, 1958), where Mills asserts that "The thrust toward World War III is *not* a plot on the part of the elite, either of the U.S.A. or that of the U.S.S.R. Among both, there are 'war parties' and 'peace parties,' and among both are what can be called crackpot realists. These are men who are so rigidly focused on the next step that they become creatures of whatever the main drift—the opportunist actions of innumerable men—brings" (pp. 93–94).

18. For Irving Fisher's observation, and others of the same sort, see Charles H. Hessian and Hyman Sardy, *Ascent to Affluence: A History of American Economic Development* (Boston: Allyn and Bacon, 1969), p. 628.

19. There are some apparent exceptions, such as Lester Thurow. But Paul Samuelson, the Irving Fisher of this era, is not one of them. For example, in an interview for *La Repubblica* (Italy) (May 13, 1987), Samuelson expressed the view that a sufficiently lowered dollar would rectify the U.S. trade deficit and that such a movement would be "good for everyone." That increased exports for the U.S. with reduced imports would mean decreased exports for the rest of the world (as they face increased competition) must surely be known by the dean of U.S. economists; but his comment ignores that reality, as it does many other realities. On the same day, in the same journal, the head of Italy's central bank said, "The chaos will continue until America puts its house in order," while making it clear he expected no such plan.

20. A broad choice among books for study and adaptation will be given. Among them, Alan Wolfe, *America's Impasse: The Rise and Fall of the Politics of Growth* (Boston: South End Press, 1981), provides both an analysis and a set of policy recommendations that, though different from mine, are complementary and harmonious.

CHAPTER 2

The Capitalist System: Ideology, Imperatives, Realities

Origins, Principles, and Dynamism

Capitalism as a socioeconomic system first appeared irreversibly in Great Britain about two hundred years ago and spread from there to what became the "major powers" by the end of the nineteenth century. Those nations became major and powerful because they had become capitalist. The minor powers were under the formal or informal rule of the industrial capitalist states, all functioning within the framework of a British-dominated world economy.[1]

The world and capitalism have changed greatly since those beginnings. Both because and despite all that, despite even the revolutions and other upheavals of the twentieth century, capitalism remains the dominant socioeconomic system in the world. Behind the innumerable changes of, let us say, the past hundred years, what is it that has endured and that constitutes the continuing meaning of the capitalist system?

Its basic institution is the private ownership and control of the means of production (that is, of the means of life) and the use of that property (mines, mills, fields, equipment, mineral resources) to make individual or corporate profits. As with other social systems, capitalism came into being within the guiding framework of a supporting ideology, a set of sociophilosophical assumptions and arguments, an ethic, and an associated culture, sociology, and politics. Unlike other social systems, capitalism as a system of production has had the unique power—and the need—to subordinate all social relationships and processes to its economic dynamic: the ceaseless chase after profits and power.

That capitalism has had the ability to move so forcefully through time, to sweep away all tradition, all "fixed, fast-frozen relations, with their train of ancient and venerable prejudices and opinions" (in the words of the *Communist Manifesto*), stems from the fact that it has been the only socioeconomic system ever in which it has been assumed that a society without any guidance or control—from government or church or whatever—could thrive, be safe, and enjoy well-being. It was Adam Smith, in his *Wealth of Nations* (1776), who provided the rationale for such a development. That it was a strikingly novel, not to say shocking, notion in his time (as it has become for many once more, in the twentieth century), was eloquently expressed by R. H. Tawney, when he wrote: "to found a science of society upon the assumption that the appetite for economic gain is a constant and measurable force, to be accepted, like other natural forces, as an inevitable and self-evident *datum* would have appeared to the medieval thinker as hardly less irrational or less immoral than to make the premise of social philosophy the unrestrained operation of such necessary human attributes as pugnacity or the sexual instinct."[2]

But Smith's ideas were not put before the medieval thinker; they were written for a very small audience, largely British, in the sweeping early years of the industrial revolution, and in the context of a society straining to move ahead economically within a context of pervasive corruption that perpetuated inefficiency and effectively held back innovation. Smith's audience, a motley group of incipient capitalists and their supporters, was small, but it was on its way to power and in need of a rationale to facilitate its efforts.

I shall argue that the three imperatives of functioning capitalism are exploitation, expansion, and oligarchic rule. Smith did not push for any of these as such, but the arguments he did make helped to alter British society not only so as to allow those needs to be met but also to foreclose the possibilities for any other set of social arrangements. Thus, Smith did not *advocate* labor exploitation (who ever has?), but in his day, when the labor force was demoralized, impoverished, and massively unemployed,[3] he, albeit unintentionally, provided a strong rationale for increased exploitation. Smith had intended to make a principle of the systematic elimination of both social constraints on employers and social expenditures for the poor (a principle enunciated in our time once again by Ronald Reagan and Margaret Thatcher).[4]

Labor exploitation of course had been common throughout history and was widespread and well known to Smith. But so intent was he on brushing aside the mercantilist policies holding back industrialization that he, like so many others who have been strong advocates of social change, allowed his vision to exclude unpleasant possibilities. As an earnest advocate of a system still in its formative stages, Smith may be forgiven somewhat for his errors of omission; the same cannot be said for the latter-day Smithians and their aloofness not only to possibilities but also to a long and gruesome history.

Regarding the imperative of oligarchic rule, Smith was quite clear. In arguing for the effective abolition of the role of the state in the economic (or any other part of the social) process, Smith was also arguing for the effective rule of property owners, a small fraction of the population. He saw the principal (almost the sole) role of the state as being the protector of that propertied class:

> Whenever there is great property, there is great inequality. For one rich man, there must be at least five hundred poor, and the affluence of the few supposes the indigence of the many. The affluence of the rich excites the indignation of the poor, who are often both driven by want and prompted by envy to invade his possessions. It is only under the shelter of the civil magistrate that the owner of that valuable property, which is acquired by the labour of many years, or perhaps of many successive generations, can sleep a single night in security. . . . The acquisition of valuable and extensive property, therefore, necessarily requires the establishment of civil government.[5]

In his economic analysis Smith contradicted himself with regard to "the labour of many years" as the source of wealth (for he, like Ricardo and, subsequently and devastatingly for the theory, Karl Marx, saw labor *alone* as creating "value"). However, neither he nor his followers allowed his contradiction to disturb the general recommendation that the state confine its efforts to protecting property, to the military, and, in a minor way, to education and roads. Just as he did not advocate "exploitation," but provided arguments that had that result, neither did he advocate "oligarchic rule." He did advocate rule, in effect, by the tiny percentage of the population that, in having the power to make unhindered decisions as to what to produce, how, when, and why, in the principled absence of any other decisionmaking group, would *be* an oligarchy of power.

Matters are different for Smith with reference to the third of the "imperatives": expansion. Smith not only advocated this but also, through the success of his ideas, very much facilitated its realization. I shall show that of the three needs that must be met if capitalism is to thrive, even to survive over time, expansion is the linchpin, or to put it differently, there may be endless exploitation and increasingly tight rule, but without expansion the whole capitalist process and its surrounding institutions fall into a shambles. This is true for many reasons, not the least of which is that the process of economic expansion effectively camouflages the necessary inequities and inequalities of income, wealth, and power that are intrinsic to the system.

Smith, who lived at a time when, despite outworn and obstructive mercantilist institutions, trade and technology and industrial development were all moving ahead, correctly believed that in abolishing all constraints, subsidies, Crown-granted monopolies (in trade, industry, and finance), and assorted rules and regulations, the dynamism of the time, combined with the propertied class's promotion of its selfish interests, would bring about rapidly increased and sustained economic expansion and rising productivity. What would protect the public interest from the rapaciousness of these selfish interests? The answer was, of course, contained in Smith's famous "invisible hand" of free-market competition. Smith did not foresee that the Crown-granted monopolies, which he rightfully disdained and effectively helped to dismantle over time, would be replaced by monopolies arising out of the combination of large-scale business units accompanying modern industrial production with their necessary and pervasive replacement of destructive (from their viewpoint) competition by one form or another of monopolistic arrangement. None of the Smithians today has yet risen to the level of realistic analysis allowing comment on, let alone criticism of, the existence today of monopolistic structures that far overshadow those of the eighteenth century.

But much more must be said about expansion, for as I suggested a bit earlier, expansion is the key process, the sine qua non of the entire capitalist process. That this is so requires a somewhat prolonged discussion, for although economic expansion, unlike exploitation and oligarchic rule, is almost universally viewed with favor in the present day, at all levels of contemporary society, its whys and wherefores are just as universally left unexplained—just as, we might say, everyone knows that breathing is essential, but knowledge of the details is left to the medicos. As the world economic crisis persists and deepens, however, we must become the medicos.

The Logic of Expansion

Throughout the history of capitalism, economic and political power has been held and used by a small class of owners of the means of life and by those of the same persuasion. That is, access to an exploitable labor force and to political rule has been a "given." Next, the prime need of the capitalist system is economic expansion (technically, capital accumulation). In turn, this need for expansion may be explained in terms of half a dozen underlying and interacting needs:

1. Production is for profit, not use; it is production for sale, for the market. Although profits may be made possible by labor exploitation in the production process, they can be realized only in the market by sale. The realization of profits thus depends upon market buoyancy, on the

relative scarcity of commodities' supply compared to their demand, which of course gives sellers relative power over buyers. In turn, the most generally beneficial and acceptable basis for such scarcity (as compared to natural disasters or monopolistic restrictions of supply) is the overall expansion of the economy, brought about by and further contributing to expansion in productive capacity (that is, by real net investment).[6]

2. Capitalism rests upon individualistic ownership, control, and direction of production and upon capitalist competition within and between industries and national economies, also in the era of monopoly capital. But there is a major difference between competitive and monopoly capitalism: Competition in the earlier era led to *falling* prices and perhaps to expanding markets, whereas at present in established industries it leads through "nonprice competition" (advertising, sales promotion, constantly changing appearances) to *higher* prices, thus increasing the need for expanding markets. Also, if the disproportionalities and gluts that unavoidably arise from unplanned production are to be kept within bounds, and if the sharp edges of domestic and international competition are to be blunted, expanding markets are required.

3. Technological innovation (in both products and techniques), a natural and accelerating process in industrial capitalism, requires market expansion if the increased production and productivity that make technological change profitable are to occur. In addition, the most vital part of such innovation takes place in and most affects the capital goods industries, the heart of an industrial economy (machinery, electrical products, metallurgy, chemicals, heavy transportation). These industries depend squarely upon expansion in the rest of the economy (as well as in their own interdependent sectors) if they are not to suffer losses through excess productive capacity.

4. Capitalist exploitation and accumulation depend upon and perpetuate a highly unequal distribution of income and wealth. While the mass of the population lives at levels of socially defined subsistence, a small minority is able to consume and save at relatively high levels.[7] If net capitalist savings are to be positive in their economic effects, they must be matched by the continuous expansion of real investment, by increases in productive capacity. That only takes place in the expectation of profit, which is to say, in the context of actual and expected market scarcities—in turn dependent upon expansion.

5. Capitalism has always depended to some degree upon debt financing for its production and investment activities. Such dependence has increased over time (and spectacularly since World War II) and extends throughout all spending activities—of consumers and governments, of working and investment capital. Debt financing is in the 1980s based increasingly on short-term (under one year) borrowing, which requires

even more rapid expansion of sales and jobs to provide the corporate and personal incomes and rising real tax base necessary to support markets and to refinance (or further expand) debt. The legend of the sorcerer's apprentice comes to mind.

6. From its beginnings, capitalist economic expansion has depended upon intermittent and deepening waves of *geographic* expansion. Increasing access to exploitable cheap labor, nonhuman resources, and more markets has lifted the volumes of trade, investment, and production for the core economies. This has allowed the maintenance and increase of profits and, in raising the level of socially defined subsistence, has helped to blunt social conflict in the core countries at the expense of the external populations. There have undoubtedly been sociopsychological consequences of this imperialism (taking the form, for example, of attitudes of superiority and vicarious power), which, in association with the cultivation of patriotism in the nation-states of capitalism, have also contributed to their political stability. Anything that might do so is welcome in the capitalist process, given the potentially explosive nature of its distributions of income, wealth, and power.

The interaction of *all* the foregoing defines capitalism's dependence upon continuous expansion; as the interaction of the need for expansion with the need for a weak labor force and strong minority control defines the fundamental basis for the existence and the survival of capitalism. The recurring inability of global capitalism throughout much of its history to fulfill all its needs in adequate and timely combination provides the major explanation for its tendency toward intermittent economic crisis and toward internal and international conflict.[8]

Economic expansion reduces social conflicts over the distribution of income, and the reduction of social conflicts helps the system to expand even more. The experience since World War II has been spectacularly successful in these respects for North America, Western Europe, and Japan; it is the record of sustained and widespread economic expansion that explains the reduction of class and international conflict (between the major capitalist nations) after the 1950s. But once economic expansion began to decline, in the 1970s, all kinds of troubles began to surface. What allowed the buoyancy of the postwar period were the numerous changes of its early years; by the 1970s, those changes had seen their day. If the world is to exit from the current crisis without catastrophe, capitalism will once more have to undertake and undergo substantial structural changes in production, consumption, and trade.

Capitalist Appetite and Diet, Then and Now

The crisis of the 1970s and 1980s, as was true of the deepest crises of the past, is a consequence of the particular ways in which capitalism produces its achievements, the ways and means associated with its great economic strength. It is of the very essence of industrial capitalism's processes that it would create the conditions of production and productivity that would allow the economic surplus to grow—absolutely, relatively, and increasingly.[9] Though in different terms, this indeed had been the fond hope of Adam Smith, who saw the long-run future of his "system of economic liberty" as ultimately benefiting the multitudes upon whose terrible exploitation capitalism's success depended in its period of youth and early maturation; but the laissez-faire social institutions sought by Smith and created in the nineteenth century did not allow that benign outcome. By the twentieth century, the problem became, not how to generate a growing economic surplus (Smith's focus), but how to use it (more exactly, how to sell it profitably), the focus of Keynes.

The first half of this century saw a bloody confirmation of the failure of capitalism to change itself so as to be able to absorb modern industrialism's enormous capacity to produce economic surpluses. The ideology and institutions of competitive capitalism, the system that prevailed up to World War I, had become as anachronistic as the metallurgy of Smith's time.

When capitalism came back to life after World War II, it did so within the new framework of monopoly capitalism, dominated by the United States even more than the earlier system had been by Great Britain. What made the system work so well in the twenty years or so after 1950 were the institutional means it developed for simultaneously generating and absorbing an ever-rising economic surplus, whose size and composition made the economic achievements of the nineteenth century seem quite puny by comparison.[10]

Capitalism's triad of needs continued and had to be met; indeed, for them to be satisfied, monopoly capitalism had to go farther and faster and deeper than its predecessor. Labor exploitation within the leading capitalist nations lessened—the other side of rising per capita consumption of goods and services and improved working conditions (health care, pensions, and so forth). However, just as Britain's immensely profitable empire had enabled it to lower its internal exploitation rates in the half century or so before 1914 (also under the pressure of organized labor), so in the post–World War II period the increased and broadened areas of exploitation in the neocolonial world made it possible for average real per capita consumption to rise dramatically in the rich nations. Such consumption rose not only painlessly for business but also, because of associated rapid expansion, quite profitably. Moreover, capital has been able to increase its profitability also through the exploitation of consumers through monopoly pricing and of taxpayers by reason of the disproportionate benefits accruing to capital when compared to its tax payments.

The expansion of consumption and investment within the leading economies and the expansion of world trade and investment over the entire globe were more rapid, pervasive, and sustained in the recent period than ever before, and given the sociopolitical complexities of monopoly capitalism when compared to the relative simplicities of its parent, rates of expansion had to be so. To have a pie with large and growing slices for labor *and* capital *and* the state, all at once, the pie had to become very large, very fast; and when one considers that the growth of appetites was also an integral part of the magic of the new system, the growing need to expand is easily comprehended.

Exploitation lowered but spread, and expansion both accelerated and spread in the new era. What about oligarchic rule? A paradox suggests itself: The politics of monopoly capitalism within the major powers is in a real sense more democratic than in the earlier era, at the same time that there is also a greater concentration of both economic and political power. This points to an increase in the sophistication of those in power and in their ability to use public relations techniques. But by itself that increase would have meant little without a real basis, the vital, noncodified but nonetheless real "agreement" between labor and capital (discussed later in this chapter) that underlay changes beneficially affecting almost the entire population, changes associated with consumerism, the welfare state, and the like. The process may be seen as a modern version of noblesse oblige or, in its U.S. manifestation, as "corporate liberalism."

All these changes in the functioning of capitalism as an economic system caused changes in the ideological realm as well, in partial but critical ways: (1) the activist state of today may be compared with the minimal state of Smith and the rhetoric and beliefs associated with each of them; (2) the militarization of the economy and of foreign policy for (among others) the United States constituted a striking about-face when compared with the pre–World War II period. It is now virtually forgotten (but not by the military) that antimilitarism was ubiquitous in the 1920s and 1930s; that, for example, expenditures for the U.S. Post Office exceeded those for the military in the 1920s (and the postal service was comparably superior). We may terminate (but not exhaust) the changes in ideology by pointing to (3) consumerism and its supports. Before World War II, numerous homilies (which had begun to erode for the top levels in the 1920s) were taken as gospel in the United States: "A penny saved is a penny earned." "Neither a borrower nor a lender be." "Waste not, want not." And so on. Many people under fifty in the United States have never even heard of these one-time axioms; and if repeated on, let us say, the Johnny Carson show, they would generate belly laughs. Even more, if these principles were put into practice, the economy would collapse.

Now we must look more closely at the post–World War II capitalist system, examine its institutions, policies, and structures, in order to understand what has made it work well when it did and what has taken it into crisis more recently.

Monopoly Capitalism in Growth and Decay

As a classification for contemporary political economy, "monopoly capitalism" is not, of course, popular usage; a brief comment on its applicability is thus in order. The term itself is not the issue, but it is important to acknowledge the indisputable and major characteristics of today's capitalist system. These have little in common with the explicit and assumed characteristics of competition and laissez-faire that alone give credence to the central precepts of conventional political and economic theory; even less are they suited to the reemerged and rising importance of competitive capitalist rhetoric ("free market" this, "competitive" that and the other) heard most often in the United States and Great Britain, but also in an almost comical fashion in Germany, France, and Austria, and most bizarre of all—in Japan.

Monopoly capitalist society is one whose structures are dominated by the centralization and concentration of almost everything that is valued in the society, but especially of power; in almost all aspects of social existence, but most clearly in the economy and over state policies. The concentration of economic power is the dynamic core of the system. That core is surrounded by a complex set of supporting structures and processes, most important of which are those embodied in the growth, the concentration, and the uses of congenial state power, all essential to meet changing economic, political, and social needs as well as to cultivate the national and global opportunities of monopoly capitalism.[11]

Given the two dynamic and interlinked centers of power, the super-corporation and the superstate, monopoly capitalism created and depended upon several other developments: the strengthening and spread of consumerism; the re-creation of an integrated capitalist world economy and empire, under the leadership of the United States (not Great Britain, as earlier); the concomitant growth of a "military-industrial complex" and "military Keynesianism," along with a spectacular growth of private and public, national and international indebtedness; and, required and facilitated by *all* these changes, the extension and refinement of the techniques of mass communications for commercial and political exhortation and manipulation. Mass communications became the lubricant of monopoly capitalism, of its managed minds and markets, its managed everything. It is a high tribute to these techniques that the rhetoric of market capitalism and democratic rule spread into the minds of a disinformed population at the same time as the troublesome realities of monopoly capitalism and contemptuous oligarchic rule increasingly dominated that population's daily existence.[12]

It all held together and worked more or less smoothly for a notable period of time. The years after 1950 until the early 1970s were the most broadly successful in the entire history of capitalism, as measured by the ways in which the system's basic needs were met. Expansion manifested itself in all areas of economic activity: in per capita consumption, especially in the leading countries and in consumer durables; in all aspects of real investment, in all forms of construction and equipment and all areas of productive capacity; in striking technological changes at all levels and in all sectors, in product and techniques, in industry, agriculture, and services, in matters trivial and fundamental; and in enormous increases in trade and investment.

In the major nations the economic surplus grew so rapidly and reached such levels that it became both possible and necessary to have not only guns and butter but also welfare—for a while. A key adjunct to this process, from the 1950s on, was a de facto agreement between capital and labor, requiring cooperation with the state, a pact that subdued class conflict: (1) capitalists enjoyed the right to do what they would, when and where and how they chose, with support or at least acquiescence from (in the United States) the trade union movement and (in Europe) the Left, up to and including imperialist adventures, whereas (2) "labor" could expect real incomes to rise in keeping with (or sometimes in excess of) increased productivity, could expect a low ceiling on unemployment and a floor beneath the lowest incomes, along with health and welfare benefits, and could expect union security and a selective access to political power. As class conflict was suppressed or abandoned, socialist aspirations dimmed or were extinguished. The economic and political bargaining of organized labor and most of the Left, at least tacitly and often explicitly, accepted capitalism as permanent.[13]

In the United States there were of course the numerous and widespread uprisings of (mostly) students and blacks. These were aimed at social, political, and military, rather than at narrowly economic, targets for the most part. These struggles had many positive consequences: Blacks and other minority groups did achieve significant political gains; the draft and the war in Vietnam both ended, and it is unlikely that either would have happened as and when it did without substantial protest. Subsequent struggles were modeled at least in part on those of the 1960s. In fact, the mighty edifice of regenerate capitalism trembled noticeably for a while. As the 1970s wore on, conflicts within and among the various struggling groups, abetted by help from the Federal Bureau of Investigation (FBI) and other such agencies, allowed social protest to dwindle, even though economic troubles were growing and spreading. After a stormy period beginning in the early 1960s, the era may be seen as one of essential social and political stability in the United States and the other major capitalist powers.

In the Third World, however, attempts to break free from the distant and recent past came to have grave and cumulative effects, to be examined in later pages. The process of liberation, begun in India, Indonesia, and China in the 1940s, was accelerated in the 1950s in North Africa and the Caribbean. As the 1960s began, the many decades of struggle in Indochina came to a head, and by the time the 1970s had ended and the 1980s had begun, old or new struggles in Africa were concluded or headed toward climax, while rumbles became explosions in various parts of Asia, the Middle East, and Latin America. The legacy of the old imperialism combined with the deeper penetration of the new, and the consequent debts, threats, and promises, have now made for an unavoidable and quite probably unstoppable process of divorcement, no matter how, no matter where, no matter why or what. For reasons to be examined in the next chapter, the weakening or severing of the many ties between the Third World and the major capitalist nations has exacerbated old problems. It has also made it much harder for the United States, with the cooperation of Britain, Germany, and Japan, to maintain the integrated world economy so necessary for the strength of the capitalist process.

Let us return now to the center nations: I have noted that both economic and political stability after 1950 depended upon the system's ability to generate and to absorb large and always-growing economic surpluses. That ability could not persist unless there were continuing and suitable institutional changes that would enliven the structures of production and trade. While the system is expanding, the need for change does not surface; when expansion slows, as recently, the kinds of changes that become likely are also inappropriate: They are defensive, combative, or protective in nature, and they help to make a bad situation worse.

As was touched upon earlier, the time of troubles heralding the chronic crisis of the late 1980s began in the early 1970s: breakdown of the international monetary system, after 1971; slowdown *and* inflation, 1970–1972; higher inflation in 1973 *and* severe recession, 1974–1975 (the worst recession since the 1930s); the oil shocks beginning in December 1973, as the oil-exporting countries (led by OPEC), importers of products from the inflating industrial countries, sought to escape the consequences of higher prices from others by raising their own.

By early 1973, inflation was at 7.5 percent in the United States and double-digit almost everywhere else (three-digit in most Third World countries), and unemployment was rising all over the globe. Inflation began to subside in the 1980s, but that was made possible by the deliberate, harsh contraction of the U.S. economy in 1981–1982,[14] both deeper and more pervasive than that of 1974–1975. Along with these economic contractions and inflations of the late 1970s through most of the 1980s, and at least partially caused by them, were increasing "violations" of the labor-capital truce alluded to earlier. Aided by the state and increasingly conservative governments, business sought to hold the line on profits by pushing down its wage and tax costs, indifferent to or unaware of a major consequence that would result—the weakening of consumer markets.

In addition to a steady erosion of social benefits and increased taxes for lower- and middle-income groups, labor found its real wages declining through most of the 1970s and 1980s, its unions lacerated and decimated, and unemployment high and growing (rates varying from country to country, but at historic highs except for the 1930s, and persisting). All this has happened with barely a peep of outrage from organized labor in the United States and dramatically little from the political Left in Western Europe, which, having cooperated in quieting the voice of workers, now seemed unable to learn to speak politically again.[15]

An examination of the functioning of the world economy will show that the manner in which the United States lifted itself out of recession in 1983 and served as "locomotive" to the world economy may well turn out to have been a deadly cure. But first one must analyze developments within national economies, remembering that what may be analytically useful may not be realistically possible: The world economy and national economies are inseparably linked.

The Failures of Success

It may be argued that in the early years of monopoly capitalism's development it was the relationships and processes within, more than between, nations that were the keys to its achievements and, as well, the bases for the critical and extraordinary expansion of world trade and investment (which, of course, supported and enriched the national developments). In the years after 1970, however, it has been the functioning of the world economy that has come to be critical and to dominate the system's economic and political processes. And as the national developments were in some sense independently creating diverse forms of national crisis, these were made all the more stubborn by what increasingly has become a malfunctioning world economy. As James Cypher put it, "The 1960s and 1970s witnessed a fundamental transition—from a world dominated by Keynesian forms of national economic management to a world system dominated by the anarchy of global competition."[16]

Among the leading capitalist societies, the United States became the most fully realized monopoly capitalist system, but all of the principal nations followed suit to an important degree or had earlier moved somewhat along the same path. U.S. monopoly capitalism was in fact a pastiche of developments elsewhere (for example, the role of militarization cum welfare in pre–World War I Germany) as well as an extension of developments hitherto unique to the United States (such as the beginnings of consumerism before World War II).

What made monopoly capitalism work well was the close interaction and mutual support of *all* its major elements in their post–World War II forms: the supercorporation and superstate, consumerism, militarism, the world economy and imperialism, deep, pervasive, and always-rising indebtedness, and the facilitating mass communications system. It is vital to recognize that it has been developments within these elements that have caused the system to settle into chronic crisis. Not for the first time in history, a social system has done itself in as it suffers the defects of its virtues. This should be evident as we explore the transformation in function of the major elements of the system.

First, we may take some samples from the central core of monopoly capitalism, the interdependent supercorporation and superstate. Their unavoidable consequence was an expansion of private and public bureaucracies. In the early years, such bureaucracies more than "earned their keep" through organizational techniques that allowed massive structures to grow and to thrive and to enhance their incomes and power. More recently, however, these same bureaucracies, still growing, have become counterproductive, marked as they are by heedless expansion, notable wastes and inefficiencies, and often striking declines in productive activity—providing the media with material for a steady chorus of lamentations.

Among the careful observers is *Business Week*, which, in March 1986 for example, cited some of the most recent and energetic achievements of the supercorporations: (1) the "hollowing out" of U.S. industry, (2) the enormous amounts of time and money that increasingly go into takeovers and the resistance to them, and (3) the already great and always-increasing emphasis upon financial speculation at home and abroad. Their combined effects include fewer industrial jobs, upward pressure on interest rates, volatile and obstreperous foreign exchange rates, and, to be treated later, a fragile and explosive international financial system—all this either viewed congenially by the superstate or beyond its control.[17]

The superstate has its own bureaucracies, of course. Although they are encumbered with different defects, they need merely to be mentioned to remind one of the bureaucracies' follies, inefficiencies, and costs— most grievously as well as most importantly those associated with the Pentagon. Attention is paid to its $700 toilet seats and $2,000 screwdrivers, but these are not (alas!) anything but the footprints of the beast. The Pentagon, perhaps the most powerful, effective, and among the very largest bureaucracies in history, has spent over $4 trillion since 1946 (that is, *after* World War II) for who knows what real purposes and what real consequences. These expenditures may be less decisive, finally, than its desire, its need, and its ability to sell militarism as a way of life. In this pursuit the Pentagon has been helped by the supercorporations and the politicians who also profit from this obscene, dangerous strategy.[18] By the late 1980s, both the private and the governmental bureaucracies, still essential for those who run them, serve less for the creation of new bases of economic strength, or social and global stability, than for the increasingly costly retention of what has been controlled—if it has been retained.

Also part of the foregoing, the normal practices of businesses and between businesses, politicians, and governments, classified as "corruption" (along with the pervasive dishonesty thus required), have deepened and spread to new, spectacular levels. The results include financial and political difficulties for all concerned and advantages for only those in the expanding public relations field who are paid to obscure the truth or correct blunders (as former White House Chief of Staff Donald Regan put it, "follow the horses and clean up the mess"). That the rich and powerful corrupters and corruptees who preside over leading U.S. bureaucracies are also vigorously puritanical in their public statements doubtless has some significance in itself, but I do not believe it would be worthwhile to search for it.

And then there is debt. The growth of governmental and consumer and business spending could not have taken place without extraordinary increases in the composition and the levels of debt and, less necessary but a predictable associate, the spread of dubious and dangerous financial practices within and among nations, bringing the world to the place where "casino capitalism" has become an apt description as well as a colorful epithet. The entire financial apparatus that is linked to farmers and oil, or Latin America, or savings and loan associations, or real estate, or the innumerable games of the world's securities, options, and other markets is an interdependent system whose solvency is increasingly in doubt. Its activities have become increasingly feverish and seem to be led by financial gunslingers rather than by the mythic figures of conservative outlook and pin-striped suits. Although Wall Street and its global counterparts have never been comfortable with principles that go beyond accounting statements, neither have they ever before been so much what they are now. It is finally these speculators who will take debt and its surrounding financial system to the next destination.[19]

Even consumerism, so useful in assisting both the profitability and socioeconomic stability of the system, has now become dysfunctional. The entire population of the leading countries (and a small percentage of those in the Third World) has been led to accept, to want, and in some ways to need, a level and composition of consumer expenditures that—given today's distributions of income and purchasing power—are quite simply beyond the present or potential income capacities of a good half of the populations of the rich countries. With consumer indebtedness now at all-time highs in absolute and relative terms, it would seem that the debts of consumers have joined the public and foreign debts of the United States and the foreign debts of the Third World as being no longer a basis for expansion, but a basis for disaster. The change is a result of the slowing down of economic expansion: Consumers borrow more, although their incomes have ceased to rise proportionately; the United States borrows more at home and abroad, despite and because its economy grows weaker; Third World economies borrow more simply to pay interest, as their exports *and* their imports decline, as their prices and their unemployment rise. And to this one must add the precarious changes in corporate financing that have occurred and that are marked increasingly by soaring debt characterized by short-term liabilities.[20]

Consumerism, which depends upon rising expectations along with rising incomes, has altered the popular definition of "subsistence," that is, what is economically necessary to keep the economic and social peace. But at the same time, because of its functional associations with large-scale economic waste, the economy has become unable to provide that level of consumer expenditures for most of the people. There is something else: Subtly but integrally associated with consumerism there has been an alteration of normal human desire and selfishness into a kind of twisted "individualism" going through and beyond greed. Not only does this exacerbate the instabilities of a society of "greed and glitz," but it also depends upon a certain narrowing of the always-tunnellike social perspectives in capitalist society.

The consequences this process has had and will have on the political processes of the United States and elsewhere cannot be known, but they do not augur well. All this has occurred at a time when the people need their social wits about them as never before both to stay out of war and to hold off or move away from economic misery.[21]

The dysfunctioning of consumerism is not caused by the inequality of income as such (although recent increases in inequality are significant). Inequality of income, of wealth, and of power are essential to capitalism; without them, capitalist profits, ownership, and direction of the social process are unthinkable. That dysfunctioning has occurred in the late 1980s because of the very high and always rising levels of systematic waste: in monopoly capitalism's advertising, sales promotion, packaging, incessant product change (largely in appearances), in its deliberate obsolescence, and in the accompanying vast waste of labor, materials, and equipment, in its vast bureaucracies, in its always more restricted agricultural and industrial production, and, among other areas and most draining, in its military production.

Taken together, these and other areas of waste require a *lowering* of the definition of socially necessary subsistence, a level that has risen so much since the 1950s. Despite appearances to the contrary, that lowering has been under way now for more than fifteen years, as measured in after-tax real per capita income.

If one were to deduct from the GNP the amount that is military, average income would fall substantially more than official figures now show. Waste in the military realm, in both expenditures and adventures, deserves special attention because it is the most substantial area of waste and because it is the conversion of military production to human needs that can most easily provide a vital basis for beneficial change.

Military waste is not only pure waste but also very large-scale waste of scarce raw materials, advanced technology, and valuable skills, as well as an increasing interest burden for private and public borrowing. *Item:* During the oil panics of the 1970s, it became known that the Pentagon was the eighth largest consumer of oil in the world—after the United States, Britain, France, Japan, the Soviet Union, Germany, and Italy. All other nations used less oil than the U.S. military. The several trillions of dollars of military expenditures in the United States *after* World War II have been intermittently useful and necessary in preventing recessions from getting out of hand, as military expenditures were indispensable in ending the depression of the 1930s. Thus the United States has had "military Keynesianism."[22] The reasons why military expenditures are so stimulating is that they increase the incomes of those in military production but do not increase marketed products in competition with others. That also makes them the most inflationary kind of spending.

Not only has military spending risen dramatically in the past decade in real terms, in that same period it has ceased to be the effective job creator it once was. Today's high-tech military dollar funnels into a relatively few corporations and the highest levels of the labor force:

fewer jobs for the buck, whether or not there is "more bang for the buck," as has been claimed in the past. As the economic stimuli of the military are losing their punch, its major functions of containing anti-capitalist and anti-imperialist movements in the world also seem increasingly, though not totally, dubious, quite apart from the dangers and the horrors associated with such a policy.[23]

Finally, in this somber catalogue of what is going wrong with monopoly capitalism, I return to what is seen as its crowning success, namely, the enormous increases in national and international real investment and productive capacity and, for a while, rising real incomes. There have been perverse effects in this connection also, perhaps the most telling of all. The growth of productive capacity has become the growth of excess capacity, yielding a constant tendency toward *stagnation* (the inability of economies to expand sufficiently to provide acceptable levels of employment and general profitability). But at the same time, the enormous increases in all forms of private and public spending created multiple pressures toward *inflation*, given monopoly pricing and the general belief that serious recession was a thing of the past.

Monopoly (more technically, "oligopoly") power allows rising costs to be passed on in the form of higher prices to buyers, whether consumers or other (especially smaller) businesses, with only token interference, if any, from the state. This is so whether the rising costs are an outcome of the global pressure on raw materials, or the capital-labor truce, or rising interest rates. *Item:* When in the mid-1970s severe recession struck, hardest of all perhaps in the U.S. automobile industry, that industry cut back on production by about one-third (thereby adding to unemployment and reducing consumer demand, of course) and raised prices on the average by 10 percent. In thus violating the precepts of conventional economic analysis, the industry was also contributing to simultaneous recession and inflation—to *stagflation*.[24] The resulting stagflation is only one of several ways in which the behavior patterns of monopoly capitalism have produced surprises for economists as much as (or more than) the general public.

Another novel set of developments has to do with the world economy and overcapacity. Because of monopoly capitalism's superstates and supercorporations, the consequences of the combination of excess capacity and competition are often surprising. Thus, while the global automobile industry attempts to deal with substantial overcapacity (the ability to produce at least forty-five million cars annually, facing a world market—at today's prices—of something closer to thirty-five million), two phenomena are revealing: (1) although there is no reason or expectation for an expansion of world auto demand even to forty million cars per year, productive capacity is increasing, not only in newly producing countries such as South Korea and Yugoslavia, but also, through changing productive techniques and locations, by U.S. companies (domestically and abroad); (2) the intense problem of Japanese auto exports to the United States received a solution in the form of "voluntary export quotas" by the Japanese (something under two million cars annually), beginning in 1982. The consequences of these two developments have been more auto imports at low prices from South Korea and Yugoslavia and about the same amount of imports from Japan, at higher prices (as the cars are "loaded" with extras, which do not discourage sales). U.S. cars also carry higher prices, as U.S. producers take advantage of higher Japanese prices to make higher profits. The companies are doing fine, but there are many fewer U.S. autoworkers, and although those laid off have found other jobs, their average earnings are less than $10,000 a year, compared with close to $30,000 previously. Well-paying and protected unionized jobs are replaced with part-time, low-paying jobs without benefits, security, or advancement possibilities.[25]

When the supercorporations pass on higher costs to small business and to the public in the form of higher prices they are setting the general direction of the economy—more so than the Federal Reserve can or does. The 500 largest industrial corporations have annual sales equal to about two-thirds of gross national product (and the giants in utilities, transportation, and other areas are similarly potent); an increase of their prices *is* inflation. One meaning of this is that a restrictive monetary policy by the Fed (one that raises interest rates to forestall or to lessen inflation, for example) is in practice likely to have the contrary effect of adding to inflationary pressures. At the same time, small business generally cannot pass on higher costs of any sort and will consequently be pushed toward contraction by that same policy, thereby adding to the always strong tendencies of big business to swallow the small.

Let us turn to the premise that capitalism, whether "competitive" or "monopoly" in its guiding institutions, cannot function well except insofar as it is global in structure and processes. In the first years of this century there were intimations of monopoly capitalism (as defined earlier) in both Germany and Japan—but only as national systems. They could not achieve the necessary global hegemony without war (or, in the event, with it), lacking, as both did, the unchallengeable economic or military supremacy needed to organize a world economy. It was the bringing into being of the post–World War II world economy by the United States that allowed monopoly capitalism as a system to function and to flourish.

In its early years, it was the capital, the arms, and the largely U.S.-designed institutions that gave the global system its life and dynamism. The United States remains the key nation in the global economy. Recently, however, it has come to play a role unique in the history of capitalism: Necessary as locomotive, it is able to play that role and to pay for its high and rising private and military consumption *only* by borrowing heavily from the rest of the world—most notably from Japan. This novel historical development is inherently unstable and cannot but be short-lived. There is no telling what the timing and the form of deepening crisis will be in the near future, but it would be reckless to assume that the world economy can or will avoid catastrophe without deliberate and basic changes. It is probable that if and when disaster nears, it will find its proximate impulses in the world economy, and the cracks will sound first from the international financial system. In the next chapter I shall try to show how and why.

Notes

1. The rise, strengthening, and decline of British industrial capitalism and the nineteenth-century world economy it dominated are definitively treated by E. J. Hobsbawm, *Industry and Empire* (New York: Pantheon, 1968). The disintegration of that world economy is examined both theoretically and historically in Alfred E. Kahn, *Great Britain in the World Economy* (New York: Columbia University Press, 1946). The more general treatment of capitalism's basic institutions and processes are usefully presented in a collection of essays edited by Richard C. Edwards, Michael Reich, and Thomas E. Weisskopf, *The Capitalist System* (Englewood Cliffs, N.J.: Prentice-Hall, 1986). Much of the following discussion of capitalist ideology and imperatives is adapted from Chapters 1 and 2 of my *Twisted Dream: Capitalist Development in the United States Since 1776* (Cambridge, Mass.: Winthrop Publishers, 1977).

2. R. H. Tawney, *Religion and the Rise of Capitalism* (New York: Mentor, 1950), p. 35. Published first in 1926.

3. All this was happening because the so-called enclosure movement (which pushed hundreds of thousands of families off the land, as agriculture was modernized) greatly reduced work on the land, but the factory movement and industrialization were not to begin to offer jobs until after 1815 (the year in which the first textile factory began). The medieval and Elizabethan Poor Laws (in which "poor" meant unemployed) required the society to provide either work or assistance (normally at the parish level); Smith's work inspired Thomas Robert Malthus, Jeremy Bentham, and others to push successfully for the abolition of those provisions (among others), in a process stretching from the 1790s into the 1830s.

4. That Smith had humanitarian purposes is convincingly shown in Eli Ginzberg, *The House of Adam Smith* (New York: Octagon Books, 1964). A masterful treatment of the basic ideas of Smith and of his times is Samuel Hollander, *The Economics of Adam Smith* (Toronto: University of Toronto Press, 1973).

5. Adam Smith, *An Inquiry into the Nature and Causes of the Wealth of Nations* (McCulloch edition, London, 1869), p. 561.

6. These generalizations and their focus upon investment are most clearly true for a capitalist process little assisted by state expenditures and taxes, as was the case especially for British and U.S. capitalism before World War I. In the present monopoly capitalist era, precisely because the capital accumulation process cannot sustain profitability (or therefore, capitalism), private capital accumulation has had to be surrounded and sustained by a "warfare-welfare" state, its taxes and expenditures, its consumerism, and its deliberate waste. All of this will be discussed later in this chapter as well as in Chapter 4.

7. In the United States, it has been typically true that the highest 10 percent of income receivers do *all* the net savings; the other 90 percent may or may not save, but their savings are cancelled out by their borrowing—without which consumer spending would of course be drastically lowered. In recent years, the national savings rate of the United States has dropped dramatically (it is anywhere from a half to a fifth of that of other industrial capitalist countries).

8. That the United States, considerably more than any other capitalist nation, has been able to find relatively healthy rates of expansion for almost its entire history goes a long way toward explaining why the politics of the United States is so different from that of Europe.

9. Paul Baran and Paul Sweezy, in their *Monopoly Capital* (New York: Monthly Review Press, 1966), have developed the idea of the economic surplus as central to the modern capitalist process. They defined it as follows: "The economic surplus . . . is the difference between what a society produces and the costs of producing it" (p. 9). The "costs" are measured by normal personal and capital consumption.

10. Ibid., focused on the interaction of the generation and the absorption of the economic surplus. See Chapter 3, "The Tendency of the Surplus to Rise," and Chapters 4–7, on the absorption of the economic surplus through "capitalists' consumption and investment," "the sales effort," "civilian government," and "militarism and imperialism."

11. Gabriel Kolko, *Main Currents in American History* (New York: Pantheon, 1984), discussed these and other developments as "political capitalism," in his Chapter 9.

12. Herbert Schiller has concentrated on this area of monopoly capitalism in illuminating ways. See, among his other works, *Mass Communications and American Empire* and *The Mind Managers* (Boston: Beacon Press, 1971 and 1973, respectively). "Military Keynesianism" is the conscious use of fiscal (that is taxing and spending) policy to counter the tendencies toward economic downturn (recession regularly, depression less so), by regulating the flow of military expenditures—something like turning the hose up or down in its flow—to do the job. Keynes deplored military expenditures and advocated what is now called social spending—on housing, roads, education, etc. See James M. Cypher, "Capitalist Planning and Military Expenditures," *Review of Radical Political Economics* 6 (Fall 1974), pp. 1–19.

13. See Michael Kidron, *Western Capitalism Since the War* (London: Penguin, 1970), Ernest Mandel, *Late Capitalism* (London: Verso, 1975), and James O'Connor, *Accumulation Crisis* (New York: Basil Blackwell, 1984), for all these developments.

14. That the contraction was deliberately wrought is generally accepted; that it was brought about exclusively through the Federal Reserve System was the argument of William Greider, in his *Secrets of the Temple* (New York: Simon and Schuster, 1987), a book well worth reading—although others, myself included, believe credit should be given where credit is also due: namely, to the Reagan administration.

15. The national and global developments are treated in three separate and successive issues of *Socialist Review*, nos. 23, 24, and 25 (1975), by Samir Amin, André Gunder Frank, and myself, and also in Harry Magdoff and Paul Sweezy, *The Deepening Crisis of U.S. Capitalism* (New York: Monthly Review Press, 1980). For many useful facts and figures, see Wallace C. Peterson, *Our Overloaded Economy* (Armonk, N.Y.: M. E. Sharpe, Inc., 1982).

16. James M. Cypher, "Monetarism, Militarism and Markets: Reagan's Response to the Structural Crisis," *MERIP Reports* 14, no. 9, Nov.–Dec., 1984.

17. "The Hollowing of America," *Business Week*, March 9, 1986, is only one of many substantial efforts by that journal to sound alarms about debt, competition, productivity, trade, and among other matters, speculation. Such feature essays appear regularly and are worth reading for both their analysis and their useful factual summaries. For a strong analysis, see Barry Bluestone and Bennett Harrison, *The Deindustrialization of America* (New York: Basic Books, 1982).

18. The long and contorted history of the militarization of the U.S. economy and foreign policy in the name of national security is comprehensively examined and analyzed in Saul Landau, *The Dangerous Doctrine: National Security and U.S. Foreign Policy* (Boulder, Colo.: Westview Press, 1988).

19. The term *casino capitalism* has been used and explained well by Susan Strange in her excellent study of international financial instability, *Casino Capitalism* (Oxford: Basil Blackwell, 1986).

20. Debt need not be a problem; it becomes one only when it is incurred not in association with appropriate earning capacity, or when its nature or its costs impair the ability to repay. That kind of thing is typical in the late 1980s for consumers, businesses, and governments. For example, the *Wall Street Journal*, February 2, 1987, in an article entitled "Deep in Hock," had several charts showing that in the period 1960–1987, the ratio of debt to GNP has risen over 20 percent, that corporate debt as a percentage of net worth has risen from under 90 to over 115 percent, that nonbusiness bankruptcies have risen from under 200,000 to over 500,000, that household debt has risen from under 25 to over 30 percent, and that interest costs as a percentage of federal spending have risen from slightly over 9 percent to just under 14 percent. Subsequently, all these percentages have worsened. If one turns to corporate debt, the picture darkens even more. In its March 15, 1988, issue, the *Journal* showed that nonfinancial corporations' debt, significantly outstripping their growth of revenues, had risen from $586 billion in 1976 to almost $2 trillion in 1987; that in a mere three years, from 1984 to 1987, their ratio of interest payments to earnings

had risen from 40 to 49 percent; that corporate debt as a percentage of GNP had risen from under 32 percent in 1976 to over 40 percent in 1987; and that corporate liquidity ratios (the percentage of cash and receivables to debt due within a year) had fallen from 90 to 83 percent from 1980 to 1987. All these figures, from private to public, individuals to corporations, reveal a growing need to borrow and a growing recklessness in the act of doing so.

21. The Census Bureau of the United States issues regular studies of income flows, under the heading of *Current Population Reports: P-60*. These showed that from 1948 through 1966, average real after-tax hourly earnings rose by over 2 percent per annum, that the increase slowed before 1973, and from then on dropped by almost 2 percent every year into the 1980s.

22. The most informative on the broad range of economic questions connected to militarization is James M. Cypher. In addition to his writings cited earlier, see "Rearming America," *Monthly Review*, November 1981; "The Liberals Discover Militarism," in Robert Carson (ed.), *Government in the American Economy* (Lexington, Mass.: D. C. Heath, 1973); and "A Prop Not a Burden," *Dollars and Sense*, February 1984. The most theoretical of his analyses is "Capitalist Planning and Military Expenditures."

23. The industrial economist Seymour Melman (of Columbia University) has been an isolated voice in mainstream academia as, over the years, he has pointed to the costs of a militarized economy: in falling productivity, structural distortions, wasted skills, et cetera. See *Our Depleted Society* (New York: Holt, Rinehart, and Winston, 1965), and *Pentagon Capitalism* (New York: McGraw-Hill, 1970). For an overall view of the main tendencies associated with militarized production, see pp. 332–349 in Edwards et al., *The Capitalist System*.

24. The most comprehensive treatment is Howard S. Sherman, *Stagflation* (New York: Harper & Row, 1977).

25. The years of Reaganomics have increased misery greatly all along the way, as signified by an increase of 50 percent of those under the official poverty line, unknown increase in numbers of homeless people in the streets and in food lines, and similar consequences from the heartless attacks on always inadequate budgets for health and education (among other matters). It began to become clear in 1982 that the Reagan administration, with the onset of soaring deficits as a result of immense increases in military expenditures along with tax cuts for those at the top, was not quite mindless. As David Stockman reported, already at that time Senator Daniel Patrick Moynihan had begun to see these actions and their deficits as a deliberate rationale for cutting social expenditures. See Stockman's *The Triumph of Politics* (New York: Harper & Row, 1986), p. 267. What has happened already is bad enough; the costs—in blighted lives and a weakened economy—of neglected health, education, and other social needs will only be learned later.

CHAPTER 3

The World Economy

Capitalism, Exports, and Accumulation

Today's capitalism stands in sharp contrast with its pre–World War I predecessor, but of course there are also strong elements of continuity in what remains, after all, a capitalist system. The capitalist developmental process, both within and between nations, has always been and must be something like a circus tightrope act: When strong, the system moves through time dynamically by going from crisis to crisis, in a process of balance gained and lost and regained, always at higher levels of technology, organization, production, and real incomes. To flourish, even to survive, this system must satisfy its strongest imperative: It must expand through capital accumulation (vertically) within national economies, and it must expand through trade and investment (horizontally) in a buoyant world economy. The need for these interconnected processes of expansion is primary to the *system;* the needs of each country's people must be, have been, and remain subordinated to the needs of capital—for better and for worse.

The capital accumulation and the exports of each nation have in common that (1) both are essential and the production of neither is purchased by consumers within the national economy and (2) both are required to maintain levels of profitability for capitalist economies. Either or both can lead to higher levels of consumption and have done so, but that is neither their purpose nor their functional consequence.

A difference between the two processes is that capital accumulation leads directly to increased productive capacity (in new or old products), perhaps to improved productivity, and therefore to the need to find new outlets for consumption, *and/or* exports, *and/or* further investment, *and/or*, as has been critical since World War II, to higher levels of government spending in order to cheapen and to support the accumulation process.[1] Exports, in contrast, constitute a use of existing productive capacity with no necessary connection with any further national economic developments, except insofar as the economy becomes habitually structured to

41

supply an export market. If this export market declines, then substantial national economic problems occur. This is not an insubstantial exception, as the reports of sinking industries confirm.

It is important also to note that just as investment is directed by and for the class of owners and controllers of capital, exports/imports are either for use in production (for example, raw materials, machinery) or for the consumption of the higher income groups in the importing nation. Thus, both capital accumulation and exports/imports, both investment and world trade, are accomplished by and for a tiny fraction of the world's population.[2]

The world economy represents therefore a kind of safety valve for what would otherwise be each nation's excess productive capacity, but the world economy is much more than that: Without it the contemporary national economies (and their potential excess capacities) quite simply would not exist. From its earliest beginnings, capitalism as a system has depended upon the existence of a growing and always more integrated global economy. The interchanges of capital and consumer goods, raw materials and foodstuffs, technology and services, finance and labor, in the global economy have served as the principal source of the dynamic and constructive imbalance that characterizes capitalism as a social, economic, and political system.

Indeed, we may say that the internal or national capitalist developments that began to take hold first in seventeenth century Holland, and that were established fully in Britain in the eighteenth and nineteenth centuries, are historically quite inconceivable in the absence of the dominant role that those countries played and gained from in the rapidly expanding *inter*national economic activities of its era. And, as Wallerstein put it,

> Three things were essential to the establishment of such a capitalist world-economy: an expansion of the geographical size of the world in question [by comparison, that is, with medieval Europe], the development of variegated methods of labor control for different products and different zones of the world-economy, and the creation of relatively strong state machineries in what would become the core-states of this capitalist world-economy.[3]

Structures and Processes of the World Economy

Also from its beginnings, such a world economy has required the clear supremacy and economic and military domination by one nation— Great Britain before World War I and the United States since World War II. The industrial and financial strengths of the dominant nation's economy nourish the growing strength of the world economy and, for a while, add to that nation's own power, in every way. But the dominant nation does more than extend its economic strength: It creates the basic structures and shapes the main processes of the world economy. Most important of all, it disciplines the always-volatile competitive and nationalistic tendencies of the member economies, whether those countries are relatively powerful or relatively weak. The chaotic interregnum of 1914–1945 resulted from the breakdown of the world system of Britain and the complicated inability of the new U.S.-dominated system to emerge.

Within the capitalist world economy there are three levels, or "tiers."[4] Tier I is occupied solely by the supreme power, which is also the prime beneficiary of the functioning world economy. Tier II includes those nations that already are or that are becoming industrialized, and whose enlarged and substantial economic benefits are paid for by a certain loss of sovereignty. Before World War I, Britain occupied Tier I; the leading European nations, plus the United States and Japan, were in Tier II. Since World War II, the United States has taken Britain's place, and the others just noted are still in Tier II—but with, as we shall see, notable differences. These two tiers are what Wallerstein called the "core-states." Tier III comprises the colonial or neocolonial, the dependent, economies. These Tier III societies, apart from appearances and a very small percentage of their people, gain nothing and lose almost everything—economically, politically, culturally—from their coerced membership in the integrated, imperialized world economy. That mainstream economists and politicians do not see the structures and outcomes in this way, especially in regard to the consequences for the Tier III societies, that instead they speak of "partners in progress" or "fostering the development of the less-developed" should occasion no surprise. But their views are thus necessarily misleading, perhaps most ominously to themselves.[5]

The principal economic successes of this capitalist world economy have also been its undoing, in past and present, for they lead to an unavoidable decline in the relative power of the dominant economy and a decline in its vital ability to provide direction and maintain discipline. The initially unchallengeable economy (Britain in the past, the United States in the present) soon comes to be challenged by the nations of Tier II, which, having bought, sold, and borrowed both capital and technology from and to the leader, steadily become more *like* the leader. Also, because they are "late comers," they have to innovate both organizationally and technologically in ways that reduce the lead and relative power of Tier I. Both types of innovation characterized Germany and the United States in Britain's heyday, as both in the 1980s most dramatically characterize Japan—but also other entire economies, such as Germany's, or particular industries from troubling upstarts presumed to be in Tier III.[6]

The consequences of these processes include a world economy increasingly beset by excess productive capacity (as supply capabilities increase more rapidly than demand, and as the rate of expansion slows), desperate competition for markets, the conflict-laden search for assured access to raw materials and investment outlets, and seemingly as a sideshow but also a structurally connected outcome, the increasing importance of global financial speculation and instability. So it was for Britain, so it is, only more so, for the United States.

So it was, so it is: But today's conflicts and competition and connected economic and political troubles are broader, deeper, and more perilous than in the earlier period. They are so because of the very different contexts within which Britain and the United States assumed power over the world economy:

1. As the first industrial nation, Britain created a world economy without, one may say, planning to do so. When the turn of the United States came after World War II, it was confronted by a world economy long in ruins; and the United States both could and had to move in planned and comprehensive (and swift) ways.

2. The United States took up its role a century or so after Britain, with all that connotes in technology and social and business organization: Britain, a nation of relatively small businesses and the technology of the first industrial revolution almost entirely; the United States, a beneficiary and creator of the second, third, and fourth "industrial revolutions" (stretching over the last quarter of the nineteenth century up to the present) and, like all the other leading capitalist nations, organized and run by giant businesses.

3. There has been a great difference in the sociopolitical culture and perspectives of Britain and the United States and associated differences in the manner and content of rule: the British, relatively cohesive, self-assured, and haughty; the United States, relatively undisciplined, self-righteous, combative, and more inclined "to go it alone."

4. Finally, the British did not face the threat, the problems, or the important political and economic *advantages* provided by the Soviet Union and subsequent successful and unsuccessful attempts of Third World countries to break loose from the capitalist system.[7]

Both the similarities and the differences between the two world economies contributed to the powerful economic expansion presided over by the United States after 1950, as they have also contributed to the alarming disruptive forces of the present world economy. A brief examination of the period of U.S. dominance and decline will show that the current situation is far from being less precarious than were affairs during the hegemony of Britain—whose decline ushered in several decades of social and physical horrors. In fact, the situation is considerably more precarious. We shall also see that what made the system work well in the recent past is what created its contemporary problems.

By the 1920s the United States was already the strongest of the industrial economies, but it did not take up that role in the global economy. When World War I broke out in 1914, the United States was $3 billion in debt to the rest of the world; by 1916 it had ceased being a debtor and had become a creditor nation; and by war's end, the rest of the world was in debt to the United States for $6 billion. The United States "enjoyed" this creditor status for the next seventy years but is unlikely to regain it. By the 1920s, the United States had taken over Britain's place as the industrial, commercial, and financial center of the world. But neither U.S. nor British foreign economic policies faced up to the new realities between the two world wars.

Economists classify nations as "mature" and "immature" debtors or creditors, as follows: An immature debtor nation owes to the rest of the world, and its imports exceed its exports; a mature debtor continues to owe, but its imports are exceeded by its exports; an immature creditor nation is owed on balance by the rest of the world, but its exports continue to exceed its imports; and a mature creditor nation is owed on balance, and its imports exceed its exports. In that last-named status, the mature creditor is allowing those who owe it to pay off their debt (or keep it from increasing unwisely) by accepting their imports. In the interwar period, the United States functioned as an immature creditor nation, and it was immature in more than the statistical sense. It behaved recklessly, for example, when Congress enacted the Hawley-Smoot Tariff Act in 1930, imposing the highest tariffs ever—the opposite of what a creditor nation should do.

A creditor nation is a net exporter of capital, a net lender to private parties and governments abroad. Debtor nations can only maintain a healthy balance in their external relationships if they can sell in the markets of the lending countries and thus earn foreign exchange. Since its Civil War, the United States has been a high tariff country, with only an occasional deviation. High tariffs were understandable until World War I, considering the mature debtor status of the United States; from then on high tariffs stood in conflict with its creditor position— until the bizarre present, when the United States is the largest debtor nation in the world, imports considerably more than it exports, and is also the largest commercial, financial, and industrial nation in the world. In this, as in other respects, all the rules of the economists' tidy world are being bent or broken.

If Britain and its free-trade policies are to be taken as the standard for the hegemonic power, then the United States was an economic lawbreaker from the moment it assumed the dominant role. Tariffs were raised throughout the 1920s and broke all records with the Smoot-Hawley Tariff Act of 1930. But Britain could *not* be taken as the standard for foreign economic policy after World War I, despite the entreaties of liberal (meaning free-market) economists from 1920 on. Why not?

First, when Britain began to rule the world economy, there were no other significantly industrialized economies. A free-trade policy maximized both exports and imports, and the imports (mostly raw materials) did not constitute a threat to British industry. But when the United States moved into dominance, it faced Great Britain, Germany, Japan, and a handful of lesser industrial nations as competitors—all, in the 1920s, hungry for export markets, all bristling with protective devices.

Second, when Britain forged its international policies, the major powers had been and would remain (relatively) at peace with each other. Britain ruled the sea-lanes, as both merchant and naval power. The United States came into supremacy in the midst of World War I, itself a result of great instability and prior conflicts. The years after the war were merely a resting period, an "armistice," until World War II. In that interim, the world was rocked by revolution in Russia and outbreaks of revolutionary and counterrevolutionary developments in the fragments of the broken Hapsburg empire; by a frenzied inflation in Germany; by fascism in Italy, Portugal, Spain, Austria, Hungary, and Germany; by worldwide depression and the collapse of colonial economies.

Had the United States pursued a set of mature foreign economic policies after 1920 (and there was no realistic possibility that it would have, given the business and political mentality of the time), some of these developments might have been slowed or averted. However, most of them would have been untouched by anything the United States might have done. It was no longer the nineteenth century. Different trading policies were needed; different policies to run an empire were needed; different policies to organize capitalist economies were needed. In sum, a world economy within the framework of monopoly capitalism was needed but, until after World War II, impossible to bring about.[8]

After World War II the United States became the effective, determined, and self-conscious architect of and ruler over a new capitalist world economy—and much more. When in 1944 at Bretton Woods the United States began to exercise leadership openly, it was uniquely strong. All the other once-powerful nations were economically, socially, and physically damaged or ruined, their imperial possessions going or gone, tens of millions of their people wounded, killed, and/or homeless. Everywhere but in the United States, capitalism was very weak and very much on the defensive.

In sharp contrast, and apart from its relatively low war casualties and total absence of war damage, the United States was blessed in every way by World War II (as earlier by World War I). It had been rescued from severe and seemingly endless depression (unemployment still over 17 percent in 1939, still over 10 percent in 1941), and it had been modernized and strengthened absolutely and relatively to all others—economically, militarily, and politically. The military and big business, both viewed with suspicion or hostility when the war began, had attained new heights of admiration and acceptance as it ended, aided in no little part by the maturing commercial and political skills of Madison Avenue (and the cinematic heroism of the Ronald Reagans and John Waynes). After 1945, neither U.S. capitalism nor its military was effectively challengeable. It was well understood in the higher circles of the United States and, grudgingly, elsewhere that the survival of world capitalism depended upon U.S. initiative and power. And given the fact that the Soviet Union was one of the most severely damaged of all nations by World War II, the threat to capitalism was not via military expansion of the Soviet Union but through the continuing socioeconomic collapse of the main structures of capitalism.

Therefore, beginning in 1944 the United States presented the world with a complex mixture of related actions and programs: (1) institutions to organize and guide national and international modernization and expansion in industry and trade (International Monetary Fund, World Bank, General Agreement on Tariffs and Trade, the Treaty of Rome); (2) financial assistance and stimulation (Marshall Plan, other governmental grants and loans) and a rising tide of U.S. private overseas investment, especially in Europe; and (3) a network of military alliances (such as NATO, Southeast Asia Treaty Organization [SEATO], Central Treaty Organization [CENTO]) entailing more than 2,000 U.S. military bases in the world and their enormous expenditures in the relevant areas (most heavily in Germany and Japan). These actions and programs, plus the blandishment, force, and threat that the United States employed, gave it the lead in creating a buoyant, compliant, and disciplined world economy.[9] It is worth adding that to the degree that the United States succeeded in its conscious efforts to diminish *national* capitalism in Europe (for example, in its promotion of the European Economic Community),[10] it also diminished the political power of the European Left: one of the several meanings of the "Americanization" of the world.

A considerable amount of the dynamism and strength of the emerging new world economy was determined by surging technological "revolutions" in such fields as transportation (jets, containerization, supertankers), telecommunications and electronics, synthetics, and petrochemicals. These developments, most often an outcome of military needs and state-subsidized research and production, meshed easily with the already-existent giant corporations, facilitating their transformation into today's supercorporations, both conglomerate (having activities in more than one industry and/or sector) and supranational, both financial and non-financial, and increasingly a mix of all these. Complementing these processes, the government in the United States pursued policies that assured domestic expansion and political stability, while also serving as prime mover of the world economy, by far the largest importer, exporter, and world investor.

The penetration of U.S. capital, influence, and power into all segments of the world economy was considerably greater than Britain's had been, and U.S. influence spread much further and more deeply than Britain's had: beyond the economic and political, into the sociology and culture of the rest of the world.

Toward Disintegration and Crisis

The trajectory of expansion of this world economy was higher and its changes more rapid and numerous than the expansion in the pre–World War I period; but what made for those differences also meant that the easy hegemony of the United States would have a relatively brief time span. After a tumultuous two decades or so, both within and between the United States and other capitalist nations, weak or strong, problems were mounting, tensions and conflicts accumulating, and crises developing.

I can only highlight the kaleidoscopic difficulties affecting or generated by the world economy. I shall do it under three headings, representative of a much broader spectrum: (1) political, military, and economic problems arising in Tier III, (2) the destabilizing consequences of contemporary technology in the context of monopoly capitalism, and (3) the role of the United States as "bull in the china shop" of the world economy.

Political, Military, and Economic Problems
Arising in Tier III

The resources of Africa, Asia, Latin America, and the Middle East have been valued by the Europeans for hundreds of years; easy access to them was indispensable to the growth of capitalism in the nineteenth century and since World War II has become all the more so. Except for what may be called the continental economies of the United States, the Soviet Union, and China, the raw materials and foodstuffs needed for an industrial country are extensively or entirely lacking (for Japan, in particular), and this is also true in critical qualitative terms even for the three giants. (To offer one example from dozens: without tungsten, which is not found in the United States, jet planes cannot be built.[11])

As world industrialization galloped from its levels of 1950 to those of the 1960s, these needs, always vital, became a matter of sheer survival. Most dramatic of all was the need for petroleum, without whose direct or indirect (as for petrochemicals) abundance, contemporary industry is unthinkable. Most of these resources are found in the needed quantities only in Tier III.

Despite their individual poverty, the Tier III nations as a group also serve as a critically important set of markets for capital and consumer goods, although this has been much vitiated by their need to pay interest on their astronomical debts and the austerity programs of the IMF. Both in the pre–World War I period and in the late 1980s, the growth of industrial overcapacity and of tendencies toward falling profit rates within the leading nations has led businesses to search ceaselessly for investments in those countries. Last, but not therefore least important, there have been compelling strategic reasons for major-power attempts to penetrate Tier III in the past and in the present. Before World War I those reasons had to do with refueling stations for shipping (merchant or naval), or gaining control of this area because it was next to that, or preventing another country from strengthening itself; even in the 1980s much or most of these reasons continue to obtain and, especially for the United States, are given added dynamism by adherence to the "domino theory"— according to which the "fall" of one country out of the capitalist orbit is but a prelude to an inexorable series of such "losses."

Naturally, all these reasons for coveting control, influence, and power in Tier III are interlocked. Taken together they have yielded an unremitting and relentless policy seeking to dominate the countries of Tier III and to forestall revolution or, having failed at that, to promote counterrevolution. After a military defeat, as in Vietnam, the policy becomes one of economic blockade. The numerous effects of these attempts to control and exploit such societies cannot of course be adequately discussed here, even briefly, but I shall deal with, among the most decisive and representative, the war in Indochina and the debt of Tier III.

The War in Indochina. Although Southeast Asia is a region rich in critical raw materials, Indochina is not. Until they were sucked into the vortex of war by the United States, Laos and Cambodia were peaceful societies that could supply their inhabitants a decent agricultural subsistence and a little more, within an ancient, beloved culture, but certainly nothing worthy of destruction. Vietnam was once rich in rubber and rice, had some coal and timber, and was of slight importance in other respects, but not strategically. The United States, however, did not invade Vietnam, Laos, and Cambodia for resources, markets, or investment outlets, or for anything economic in nature. Moreover, had it done so, its attempts to "bomb them back into the Stone Age" would have been self-defeating. The invasion took place instead for those strategic reasons. The domino theory was and is still taken seriously by many U.S. military and national security leaders and by an unknowably large percentage of the rest of the government.[12]

By 1950 as French control over Indochina had weakened, the United States began to finance the French war as a means to keep Indochina in "the free world" and, simultaneously, to secure France as linchpin for NATO (and to ensure that France would continue close cooperation with its historic and recent enemy, Germany). By 1952, the United States was footing more than half, and by 1954, four-fifths, of the financial cost of the French-Indochinese War.

To the continuing puzzlement of both the French and the United States, the French were defeated at Dien Bien Phu in 1954, and the United States commenced its long history of corrupting and destroying the people, the society, and the resources of Indochina—dropping more bombs there, for example, than were dropped by all combatant nations in World War II, to say nothing of the human and resource devastation caused by napalm, Agent Orange, and other deliberate attempts to ruin the agriculture of the area (and to transform South Vietnam from a major rice-exporting to a major rice-importing region). By 1962 there were over 20,000 U.S. troops "advising" the U.S.-created South Vietnamese Army; before the United States left Vietnam in 1975, more than 3,500,000 U.S. military personnel had done time and damage in Indochina.

All of this was of course quite costly, not only in personnel, but also in money. It became financially more costly than the simple dollar amounts spent. Beginning in 1965, in the midst of rising military expenditures including but not confined to those for Vietnam, President Lyndon Johnson was knowingly committed to a long and costly war. Unable to understand how "those little yellow dwarfs," as some officials in the administration reputedly called the Vietnamese during the war, could for long withstand U.S. might, and wishing to hide the war's true costs from the slowly awakening people, he took actions that soon aggravated the then-mild inflation in the United States, that shifted critical elements of industrial production to Japan and Germany, and that "exported" inflation to Western Europe. Johnson lied to the U.S. people about the long-run prospects of the war, and he lied to his own Bureau of the Budget about military expenditures (to an amount in excess of $10 billion), a decisive step placing taxes and expenditures into serious and cumulative imbalance—something like a ship's captain not informing his navigator of a coming storm.[13]

Johnson persuaded European central bankers to accumulate dollars, a process that has been likened to writing checks that cannot be cashed, thus promoting inflation in Europe. These events accelerated the growth of the Eurodollar market, which, as will be seen, has been and continues to be an important source of international financial instability. Financial instability and inflation were increasing even without Vietnam, but the latter sped up those processes significantly, as did, even more, what has become the spectacular and hopeless indebtedness of Tier III to Tiers I and II.[14]

Tier III Debt. Confirmation of the pervasive existence of surplus productive capacity in the leading economies may be found in the attempts of private banks to lend to Tier III countries. This process became substantially important in the late 1960s, when banking pressures were placed on (especially) the U.S. government to reduce its grants and subsidized loans in order to make room for private banks to do the lending—at interest rates that were notably higher. The search for borrowers became feverish in the 1970s, as petrodollars flooded U.S. and European banks. The main source of income for banks is, of course, the interest payments they receive on loans, and excess reserves are for them much like excess capacity for industry. When the current crisis began, in the mid-1970s, the banks could not (and still cannot) put money out at interest in adequate amounts within their own countries; consequently, they became eager hustlers of credit to most of the Tier III and to some of the noncapitalist countries, for example, Poland and Cuba.[15]

Interest rates, which were high for the borrowing countries from the outset of this process, became murderously so as inflation mounted in the late 1970s and early 1980s and moved toward catastrophe when the dollar began to soar (for all oil sales and most Tier III loans are denominated in dollars). The decline of the dollar, of inflation, of oil prices, and of interest rates in the 1980s, because the decline has been accompanied by a falling of demand and also of the export prices of Tier III, has not helped.

By now, over $1 trillion is owed to the industrial capitalist nations from Tier III, close to 40 percent by Latin American nations: the debts of Mexico, Brazil, and Argentina alone account for over half of that. All these debtor nations, including the oil exporters (and most notably, Mexico), are edging toward or have passed the point of inability to pay interest, let alone to reduce principal. As the demand and prices for their production have fallen in the world economy, these countries earn less and owe more; they are on a treadmill that takes them ever faster toward financial and economic collapse. To make matters worse, the uses to which the massive loans were put, besides high-level theft and secret Swiss bank accounts, rarely yielded projects that enhanced the debtor country's ability to repay. That such was the reality was no surprise to bank officers.[16]

The responses of the creditor nations and their banks to this aspect of the chronic crisis have been as problematic as their actions that caused the crisis, as might have been expected. U.S. Treasury Secretary James Baker's plan was to have a cooperative process of increased loans from many countries and many more banks to allow the debtor countries to ease their way through the crisis to a brighter future. But the light at the end of this particular tunnel would be furnished only by a substantial and continuing worldwide economic expansion, one in which the consequences for the debtor countries would have to be quite different from anything in the past. After all, their indebtedness was already large and rising in the "good years" of this era. The Baker Plan, like virtually everything that passes for economic wisdom in the 1980s, assumed that the crisis is an aberration and that its causes and cures are to be found in quantitative measures, rather than structural change.

The Baker Plan has found a positive, but weak, answer from the lending authorities. More effective has been the Band-Aid approach—the numerous "restructurings" of Tier III indebtedness, beginning with Mexico's in 1982. Without its ever being acknowledged as such, restructuring means that the point of default has been passed, that actual default—which in the banking world has the same quality as patricide—has been postponed, perhaps (with much luck) averted, by placing an indefinite moratorium on the repayment of principal, usually a limited moratorium on interest payments, and/or a special loan for the payment of interest and to keep the debtor country's economy functioning. This is accompanied by an austerity program: lowered social expenditures or imports and consumption and rising unemployment. These programs, designed, organized, and enforced (if at all) by the IMF, creditor countries, and their banks, do not in any way get at the roots of the problem, whether for the borrowers or the lenders. They leave untouched the recklessness and heedlessness of all concerned, who proceed still along the same lines, if a bit more worriedly, with the same structures and attitudes and the main ways and means of the world economy. Indeed, left to themselves, these restructuring efforts have largely meant two things: (1) exports to Tier III have fallen (as they must if Tier III is to be "austere"), by over one-third in the case of U.S. exports to Latin America; and (2) the failure of the first restructure leads to the second and third and fourth, a process already well on its way with Mexico, Argentina, and Brazil, among others.

Further consequences of restructuring are that the chronically softening world economy becomes always "softer" (characterized by lower rates of world trade expansion) in its production and more competitive in its trade. A connected consequence is rising financial speculation, which runs rampant within and between almost all economies of the world— including speculation in the loans to Tier III. This speculation is energized by greed and by great rivers of liquid capital that, because of pervasive overcapacity in industry, worldwide inadequate purchasing power, and tax and expenditure policies by the leading governments that exacerbate the situation, spread like a deadly oil spill into the entire world economy. And all this is speeded up and made more threatening by what we have normally taken to be an undisputed virtue: modern technology.

Technology and Capitalism

The consequences of contemporary whizbang technology have become increasingly destabilizing. Like so much else already discussed, modern technology was of course instrumental in prompting and supporting economic expansion and higher incomes. Lately, however, that same technology has begun to spell trouble, as economic expansion has slackened.

In the industrial revolution of the eighteenth and nineteenth centuries, technological development meant mostly labor-saving inventions in agriculture and industry. The technology that now moves and shakes economic life is labor saving and resource saving and capital saving. It takes place in all the nooks and crannies of the economy and, increasingly, outside the economy, for example, in education, health care, entertainment.

Both productivity and social change have been much stimulated by all these advances, doubtless more for the better than the worse. But by the late 1980s there is not a single sector (not even the fabled Silicon Valley) of the economy in which technological change means expansion. Instead, it means holding on, displacement, unemployment, bankruptcies, distress. Here, as in so much else in the capitalist process, whether a development has a positive or a negative meaning (it often has both) depends squarely upon the rate of economic expansion. As noted in Chapter 2, the needs for expansion are deep and many. Historically, a healthy rate (for the United States) has been about 3.5 percent per annum. In the 1960s the average rate was well in excess of 4 percent; in the 1970s 3 percent had become difficult; in the 1980s the tendency has been around 2.5 percent and sinking. With the rate and spread of technology in the late 1980s, it may be asserted that the healthy rate must be at least that of the 1960s, and probably, by now, even more. However, it is much less, and there is little if any likelihood of a reversal.

The seemingly endless flows of technological changes, especially those in electronics, have sped up the transformation of the world economy into one dominated by its transnational corporations, their "hollowing" effects on national economies, and by the multiplication of financial instruments, speculation, and the "instantizing" (by which electronic devices tie together all financial markets—by type and location—for immediate response) of financial procedures. All these, taken together, have placed business and governments on the verge of a financial breakdown.[17]

"Hollowing" refers to the processes by which, let us say, a U.S. clothing or automotive company farms out—"outsources"—its production to a multitude of cheap labor, tax-favorable, high-tech outlets in Tier III, with the U.S. company increasingly serving as coordinator, financier, speculator, and marketer. Meanwhile, it is also reducing its domestic work force and closing down its domestic factories. For many such companies the day has already arrived when the "farms" take on lives of their own, break loose from and become competitors of the earlier patron. Both a product of and a contribution to excess productive capacity, this process is part of another process: the tendency for finance to dominate over production.

Not only financial but also nonfinancial corporations have become part of a whirlpool of financial speculation—in foreign exchange, in futures, in options, in almost anything that can be imagined. The careers of corporate officers and their companies are increasingly seen as dependent more upon financial dexterity than, as earlier, upon production or marketing accomplishments.

There has never been a time in capitalist history when financial speculation was absent. But the periods in which it has become the main activity, as is true in the 1980s, have all ended badly. Usually, as in the years just before World War I and again in the 1920s, financial speculation grew rife alongside slowing industrial production. The outcome has been all too similar: financial crack-up that places an intolerable burden on an already weak economy and that turns slowdown into depression. The splendid excitement of Wall Street (and other exchanges in the world) in the late 1980s, the "Dow" breaking through always one more ceiling, the uncovering of large-scale scandals (like Boesky and others), are eerily reminiscent of the late 1920s, as of course, was "Black Monday."[18]

The Role of the United States in the World Economy

Now we turn to the role of the United States in this movement toward disintegration and crisis. A main theme that has run through these pages is the idea that a capitalist world economy cannot forever avoid deep crisis: In the very nature of the capitalist process, that which makes it work—the spread and increase of economic strength, for example—is also its undoing. But within that inexorable process, much variation, of rhythm, leadership, caution or its absence, for example, is to be expected. The very special history of the United States has made for a very special kind of behavior as a hegemonic power, a kind of inspired recklessness in the early years, and now a recklessness that increasingly causes shudders in the rest of the world. It is plausible to believe that this characteristic—what I earlier called "boyish"—is a consequence of the relatively carefree history of U.S. capitalism, at least as that history is viewed by its main beneficiaries.

Everything that might facilitate the emergence of capitalism and its institutions, and the progress of industry and agriculture, was there for the taking in U.S. history. No nation has matched the quantitative or qualitative abundance of natural resources in the United States, whether the reference is to climate, terrain, soils, coasts, rivers, bays, lakes, forests, or minerals or to the convenient locations of all these to each other. Nor can the vast oceans that gave the United States almost total security from invasion be ignored as a developmental advantage. Less obvious but at least as important are the temporal and social conditions within which the United States came into existence: no medieval past and thus few if any social controls to deny or destroy; a cheap—slave and free—labor supply brought in from all over the globe; a developing technology from which to borrow (as well as to embellish); easy flows of capital from Europe; and a Europe always eager to buy from the United States and to sell to it; a period in which free trade and competition were at their peaks; and a rapidly expanding world economy.

All these and many other factors meant that, except for the Civil War, U.S. history has been a story of large but easy achievements, not the kind of history to require or to produce social wisdom, self-constraint, or caution in its business or its political leaders. When Henry Ford said, "History is bunk," he was speaking for generations of those who preceded and followed him, whether in Wall Street, the White House, the media, or, for that matter, most of those in the universities. But to ignore history is to ignore the relationships and processes of society. It is to believe, and this is what is generally believed in the United States, that individual talent, energy, will, and desire are all. When there is considerable talent, such beliefs among those who rule (and are ruled) may not be entirely disastrous; when talent is ordinary or absent, however, and when social understanding (at its best, never sufficient in itself) is replaced by social ignorance, nostalgia, and bellicosity, the gods must be exceptionally kind if night is not to fall.

The gods couldn't have been kinder than they were to the United States from 1945 into the 1960s. The United States "inherited" a set of conditions after World War II that made it seem easily possible to create the world in its own image and to place much of it under its control. That leaders such as Harry Truman, Dwight Eisenhower, Nixon, Johnson, James Forrestal, the Dulles brothers (Allen and John Foster), Dean Acheson, Dean Rusk, John F. and Robert Kennedy, and Robert McNamara are given high marks for their ideas and policies, not least by academics, is a comment less on those praised than on those doing the praising. This becomes clear when one studies the intrusion of reality at the Bay of Pigs (Cuba), in Indochina, in Nixon's economic struggles of 1971 and later, in that whole range of developments neither designed nor able to be controlled by "the best and the brightest" of U.S. leaders.

When President Nixon began in 1971 to dismantle the global financial and trade system constructed by the United States a scant twenty-five years earlier, it was clear that the emperor's clothes, though not yet gone, were frayed; that Nixon was tacitly acknowledging that easy U.S. economic dominance was a matter of history, that the United States was losing its special status. That was doubtless unavoidable, but the rate of descent and the type and number of problems along the way were not foreordained.[19]

To make the case for a crisis that ineluctably moves toward disaster, neither is it necessary nor would it be correct to portray the United States as the only actor in the drama. It has not been, of course, and could not be, alone in a capitalist world economy. Some developments were initiated and controlled by the United States, others by "history" (for example, technological developments), and still others by the at least partially autonomous policies of other nations: Japan or Germany, the Soviet Union or China, Cuba or Vietnam, Israel or South Africa.

However, no important economic or military policy of the years after 1945, whatever its origin, could have taken the course it did if it had not been shaped and directed by what was once the overwhelming power of the United States, whether the reference is to Indochina, the European Common Market or Eurodollar market, the arms race, or the particular kinds of conflict and violence that have marked the Third World.[20] The United States either belonged at center stage because of its power and policies or, because of its tendency to see itself as some combination of a reborn Adam Smith and the knight Roland holding off the Saracens, it jumped out of the audience and *took* center stage.

Not that the rest of the world behaved admirably. The Europeans and the Japanese and the subservient leaders of Tier III bowed and scraped to the United States along the way. Sometimes these leaders behaved this way because they had no alternative, sometimes to save money (as in the case of military expenditures), or to make it (as in the case of cooperation with the war in Vietnam), or out of the realistic and continuing fear of economic punishment and/or military adventurism by the United States.

So the United States grinned and shouldered its way throughout the 1950s and 1960s, and only began to contemplate its mortality, if then, in the late 1970s, when President Jimmy Carter tried to strengthen the Trilateral Commission (Western Europe, Japan, and the United States) and to spread some of the responsibility (but much less of the power) over the world economy. He failed. The rhetoric of U.S. leaders from Woodrow Wilson to Truman to Reagan has always emphasized cooperation, the notion of "brothers in arms," "partners in progress," "the North Atlantic Club," and the like. The reality has been an attempt to become and to remain what the United States was in 1945: Number One.[21]

Now (the end of the 1980s) the economies of Japan and Germany are both organizationally and technologically superior to that of the United States; now with the nationally irresponsible (but in terms of profits, responsible and "rational") behavior of the supranational corporations (close to half of the top 200 of which are U.S.); now, with a technology of communications and transportation and production that gives enormous flexibility to capital (and growing impotence to labor); now, with debts at home and abroad constituting a time bomb that cannot be defused without a totally unlikely world economic expansion; now, with a U.S. government that in neither its Republican nor its Democratic representation shows much sign of social comprehension or imagination—with all that and more, the role of the United States in the world economy makes the bull in the china shop seem like Lassie at the hearth, by comparison.[22]

Meanwhile, problems spread and deepen. The world economy does not exist in a child's story, with a good fairy on the way with a magic wand that will transform dark into light. The dark consists of all that debt, all that unemployment, all that wasted productive capacity; it consists of falling real wages and rising speculation, of powerful corporations and bewildered governments; it consists of a world still dominated by an ever-weaker and poorly directed United States, still seeking to have its way in every corner of the world, heedless of what that means in terms of the national and world economies or even of war. The dark is that of the jungle and its howling animals.

We smile when someone says, "history shows . . . ," and usually with good reason. But history does have some lessons. Among them is that when a social system moves into deep trouble, it must and it will change, for better or for worse. Almost always, the worse has preceded the better, as in this century, with the "worse" breaking down social structures so as to allow needed social change. The costs already paid in the "worse" this century have been beyond calculability. Who can bear the thought of repeating and exceeding them?

What stands out today is that the present business and political leaders of the United States, Western Europe, and even Japan are all too often ignorant of the nature of both past *and* present. Faced again and again by problems, their solutions seek to reproduce an idealized past, the essence of which is to reduce the material well-being of almost all of the people in order to provide increased wealth and income to that tiny fraction of the population that has, in fact, brought us to this crisis.

Such policies may or may not have been suitable to the first stages of industrialization, when capital was scarce. In the late 1980s, capital is overabundant, given present institutions; the need is to find ways to expand consumption and production. The means to do so are at hand, and they center upon finding new ways of absorbing and adding to production instead of wasting it at the expense of the world's peoples. That the system's dependence upon waste has been immense and is increasing is the focus of the next chapter.

Notes

1. James O'Connor, *Fiscal Crisis of the State* (New York: St. Martin's, 1973), was the first to develop the political economy of the monopoly capitalist state and to analyze its dual and mutually dependent functions of "legitimation and accumulation," that is, state policies (and associated taxes and expenditures) that, largely through welfare and job creation, keep the socioeconomic peace and, through some of those and other expenditure policies (largely, but not entirely military), both condition and sustain capital accumulation. As the 1970s began, O'Connor saw a contradiction developing that would not allow *both* legitimation and accumulation to continue at the necessary levels; thus a "fiscal crisis" which would necessarily become part of a larger and deeper crisis. See pp. 1–39 and Chapters 4, 5, and 6, especially.

2. See Richard C. Edwards et al., *The Capitalist System* (Englewood Cliffs, N.J.: Prentice-Hall, 1986), pp. 99–118, for a useful general discussion.

3. Immanuel Wallerstein, *The Modern World System: Capitalist Agriculture and the Origins of the European World-Economy in the Sixteenth Century* (New York: Academic Press, 1974), p. 38. By the "sixteenth century," he meant the period 1450–1640. "Variegated labor" referred to three distinct forms of labor control: wage labor, share-cropper/tenancy, and serf/slave labor, which work in core, semiperipheral, and peripheral economies respectively—not the same as, but overlapping with, what I here call Tiers I, II, and III.

4. This designation should not be confused with "First, Second, and Third World" countries. That terminology developed out of the Bandung Conference of "nonaligned" countries in the 1950s, where the usage pointed to the powers of the capitalist (First), Communist (Second), and nonaligned world, the Third World. It was and is a political term, now much diluted by changing usage. Tier II, as used here refers to the leading capitalist powers that are *not* the dominant, or Tier I, power. The nations that presume to function outside the capitalist orbit—the Soviet Union, China, Cuba, Vietnam, and others—are not included in any of the three "tiers." This does not mean that I see them as not affected by or at all involved in the capitalist world economy; it does mean that they are not integrated into that world economy, that their participation is residual, very much partial, and quite frequently against their will. Recently, that has been changing, as some of the noncapitalist economies have seriously sought to step up trading, investment, and financial connections with the major capitalist powers as part of a long-range strategy.

5. See, among others of his books, André Gunder Frank, *The Development of Under-Development* (Boston: Beacon, 1966), for a compelling analysis of the whys and wherefores of the political economy of this process, which he has called "dependency." R. J. Barnet and Ronald Muller, in their *Global Reach: The Power of the Multinational Corporations* (New York: Simon and Schuster, 1975), showed how whatever flows to Tier III, be it capital or technology, has perverse effects there (including, always, a net flow of capital toward Tiers I and II). Among dozens of other books much worth reading, two that go beyond economics and are most valuable are Felix Greene, *The Enemy* (New York: Random House, 1970), which seeks to explain (especially to Americans) why the United States *is* an imperialist power and what that means to those who are oppressed (and, as well, to the U.S. people), and Chandler Morse et al., *Modernization by Design* (Ithaca: Cornell University Press, 1969), which approaches the process from several disciplines; best, perhaps, is Morse's discussion of the relationships between "economic" and "noneconomic" matters.

6. The reference is to the exports of South Korea, Taiwan, Hong Kong, Singapore, Brazil, and others, where cheap labor, contemporary technology, often privileged access to world markets (by virtue of their political/military role, such as South Korea) and other matters allow these countries to compete industrially. Classically, the Tier III countries were "hewers of wood and drawers of water," that is, nonindustrial, a convenient status that is no longer possible or, from the point of view of *some* capital, desirable.

7. A comprehensive study of the world economy encompassing the periods of dominance of both Britain and the United States is William Ashworth, *A Short History of the International Economy Since 1850* (London: Longmans, 1964). See also Alfred E. Kahn, *Britain in the World Economy* (New York: Columbia University Press, 1946), and Albert Imlah, *Economic Elements in the Pax Britannica* (Cambridge: Harvard University Press, 1958), as well as E. J. Hobsbawm, *Industry and Empire* (New York: Pantheon, 1968). The reference to "the economic advantages provided by the Soviet Union" seeks to underscore the uses to which the cold war has been put, both economic and sociopolitical, uses by no means confined to the United States. See the discussion in Chapter 4.

8. U.S. policies and the relevant economic data for the 1920s and 1930s may be found in Hal Lary et al., *The United States in the World Economy* (Washington, D.C.: U.S. Department of Commerce, 1943). George Soule, *Prosperity Decade* (New York: Holt, Rinehart, and Winston, 1947), and Broadus Mitchell, *Depression Decade* (New York: Holt, Rinehart, and Winston, 1947), provide not only a detailed analysis of U.S. participation in the world economy from 1917 into World War II but also the full economic history of the United States in those years. Much of the discussion of the preceding pages has been adapted from my *The Twisted Dream: Capitalist Development in the United States Since 1776* (Cambridge: Winthrop Publishers, 1977), pp. 226–233.

9. See Fred Block, *Origins of International Economic Disorder* (Berkeley: University of California Press, 1977), Michael Moffitt, *The World's Money* (London: Michael Joseph, 1983), and David P. Calleo, *The Imperious Economy* (Cambridge: Harvard University Press, 1982), all of whom, in their own ways, examined the main elements constituting the emergence of the new world economy and its subsequent processes of decline.

10. National capitalism will last as long as capitalism lasts, for complex reasons that do not need to be discussed here. But the "national" part of that system has lost much of its force as global monopoly capitalism has taken hold and functioned. This is so not only because the United States in effect usurped critical portions of the sovereignty of both Tier II and III nations—an essential usurpation if the global system were to function smoothly—but also because of the great and growing strength of the multinational, supranational corporations (among other related matters). These supercorporations not only can but in some sense must function to an important degree independently of their own and host nations; even more, their flexibility and scope make them considerably more powerful vis-à-vis any attempts by organized labor or other social or community groups to make demands upon or bargain with them, as this flexibility also weakens labor and strengthens capital in the formulation of national socioeconomic policies. For there to be political effectiveness in industrial (and related) disputes, there must be a target at which to aim. In the global monopoly capitalist world, labor's target is difficult to locate and when located, to make "sit still." One is reminded of the Oklahoma farmer (in John Steinbeck's *Grapes of Wrath*) losing his land in the days of the depression who, when his home was being crushed by an enormous tractor, sought to shoot the tractor driver. The latter, having been "tractored out" earlier himself, said it was the bank in Oklahoma City he was working for, but that the bank there was in turn controlled by a bank in New York City. "Then who'm I gonna shoot?" asked the forlorn farmer. Along with thousands of other "Okies," shortly thereafter he joined the desperate trek to California. There is no "California" to go to for those under the increasing pressures of the late 1980s.

11. See Harry Magdoff, *Age of Imperialism* (New York: Monthly Review Press, 1969). This is a valuable study in many respects and particularly useful in its analysis of the qualitative matters connected with raw materials. In 1952, President Truman's Materials Policy Commission issued a five-volume report, *Resources for Freedom* (Washington, D.C.: U.S. Government Printing Office, 1952), in which,

among other matters, the commission took the position that by the 1970s the United States would be critically dependent upon imported raw materials, both qualitatively and quantitatively, and that its foreign policies had to reflect and fulfill that need—which they were well on their way to doing. The point had been made a year earlier (1951) in the International Development Advisory Board's *Partners in Progress* ("The Rockefeller Report"), which made the explicit connection between the need for raw materials and foreign economic policy toward Tier III.

12. I sought to make the point about the relative unimportance of narrow economic considerations in the Indochina war in "The Political Economy of War," *Nation*, June 28, 1971. The larger strategic and ideological background was well discussed and analyzed by Daniel Ellsberg, *Papers on the War* (New York: Simon and Schuster, 1972), Noam Chomsky, *For Reasons of State* (New York: Vintage, 1973), and Carl Oglesby and Richard Shaull, *Containment and Change* (New York: Macmillan, 1967).

13. For this and other reportage on the 1960s in Washington, D.C., see David Halberstam, *The Best and the Brightest* (New York: Random House, 1972).

14. See Calleo, *Imperious Economy*, Chapter 3, and also the important article by Susan Strange, "International Monetary Relations," in Andrew Shonfield, ed., *International Economic Relations of the Western World, 1959–1971* (London: Oxford University Press, 1976).

15. See Susan Strange, *Casino Capitalism* (Oxford: Blackwell, 1986), and also Moffitt, *World's Money.*

16. See Howard M. Wachtel, *The Money Mandarins* (New York: Pantheon, 1986), Chapter 6, and Martin Mayer, *The Money Bazaars* (New York: E. P. Dutton, 1984), Chapter 9.

17. It seems clear that if the world economy persists in crisis with its recent slow growth rates, a recession, that is, zero or negative growth rates, even relatively briefly, would topple the extremely fragile international financial structure. It is scarcely believable that a recession is very far away, nor does it seem at all credible that reforms needed to strengthen the financial structure are likely to happen soon, if at all. As for the next recession, Leonard Silk, economics editor of the *New York Times*, has offered this view: "As things look now, three events could start a recession: a credit crunch, in which a tightening of credit by the Federal Reserve forces businesses and banks to cut their investments; a financial crisis, which could result from a Third World debt crisis, a collapse of the 'junk bond' market, bank failures, a collapse of Japanese stocks or a nosedive of the dollar; or an autonomous contraction of the economy stemming from an exhaustion of consumer spending, with real income stagnating and consumers overburdened with debt" (*New York Times*, August 29, 1987). "As things look now," it might therefore be a good time to inspect the lifeboats: Ten days after Silk wrote that piece, the Fed began to raise the discount rate as the dollar began to fall; and within three weeks of his statement there was October 19: "Black Monday." It would have been bad luck if that panicky move had become a financial collapse, but it took a bit of good luck to keep it from doing so. In the context of a recession, no amount of good luck will make a difference.

18. On "financialization," see "The Logic of Stagnation," *Monthly Review*, October 1986, wherein, among many important points, the following changes were noted: Between 1960 and 1985, GNP rose about four times, total outstanding debt about eight times, and the financial sector as a percentage of goods production rose from 29.1 percent to 40.0 percent. In regard to speculation, after 1977, industrial production rose only 25 percent, while futures speculation increased by 370 percent. In that same issue, see the useful essay by Gregory Bergman, "The 1920s and the 1980s: A Comparison," in which, after noting a few economic similarities (such as the increasing gap between rich and poor), he went on to highlight political, moral, religious, and cultural matters. Also see George Soule, *Prosperity Decade* (New York: Holt, Rinehart, and Winston, 1947) on the 1920s in general, as well as *its* financialization. For the financial debacle, see John Kenneth Galbraith, *The Great Crash* (Boston: Houghton Mifflin, 1976).

19. See Wachtel, *Money Mandarins*, Chapter 4.

20. See Strange, *Casino Capitalism*, pp. 256ff., for an articulation of this position.

21. See Gabriel Kolko, *Main Currents in American History* (New York: Pantheon, 1984), Chapter 10.

22. This condition was put forth as a *cri de coeur* by one of the more articulate and much worried stalwarts of the system, Felix Rohatyn, in his essay "On the Brink," *New York Review of Books*, June 11, 1987. See his equally vexed essays in the same journal, "The Blight on Wall Street," March 12, 1987, and "What Next?" December 3, 1987.

CHAPTER 4

Waste, Destruction, and Destructive Wastes

"War Is Production in Reverse"[1]

Nature, current technology, and existing and easily achievable productive capacities taken together could provide everything needed by all the world's people for, at the very least, their health and comfort and could do it in the reasonably near future. Instead, billions of people, about 80 percent of the world's population, go without adequate food, clothing, shelter, medical care, or education. Their lives are cruelly and needlessly shortened, cramped, and miserable, and every year many millions die horribly of starvation.

The stark contrast between what is and what could be has existed often before in history. Each time it recurs it does so at a higher level of divergence between the realities and the possibilities; each time, also, there has been an ensuing catastrophe more devastating than its predecessor. The modern era began that way, as R. H. Tawney noted sardonically:

Nourished by the growth of peaceful commerce, the financial capitalism of the age fared not less sumptuously, if more dangerously, at the courts of princes. Mankind, it seems, hates nothing so much as its own prosperity. Menaced with an accession of riches which would lighten its toil, it makes haste to redouble its labors, and to pour away the perilous stuff, which might deprive of plausibility the complaint that it is poor. Applied to the arts of peace, the new resources commanded by Europe during the first half of the 16th century might have done something to exorcise the spectres of pestilence and famine, and to raise the material fabric of civilization to undreamed-of heights. Its rulers, secular and ecclesiastical alike, thought otherwise. When pestilence and famine were ceasing to be necessities imposed by nature, they re-established them by political art. The sluice which they opened to drain away each new accession of superfluous wealth was war.[2]

Since then, the bloody sluice has been opened many more times: for "thirty years" in the seventeenth century (which, in fact, had only four years *without* war), and then intermittently in the eighteenth, rising to flood stage with the Napoleonic Wars. The so-called century of peace after 1815, when Britannia ruled the waves and the world economy, was not much of a peace for the Great Powers (including as the period did, for example, the Crimean and Franco-Prussian wars) or the United States (with its Civil War, and the war against Spain for control of Cuba and the Philippines) and no peace at all for those invaded and slaughtered by the major powers in their lust for imperial possessions.

When the "century of peace" drew to its close in 1914, history's very largest and most destructive war began, followed a generation later by the still larger, considerably more destructive war of 1939–1945. And since then, virtually continuous warfare, resembling that of the seventeenth century in its savagery and frequency, but much more damaging, has reappeared: Korea, Indochina, Lebanon, Afghanistan, Angola, Bangladesh, Mozambique, Nigeria, Nicaragua, Iran-Iraq, to take the short list.

But honors for massive waste and destruction of resources, equipment, and even of lives do not go only to war. The surrounding economic system when it is "at peace," itself a somewhat murky notion (as will be noted below), is also responsible for waste and destruction. Capitalism has been simultaneously the most efficient *and* the most wasteful production system in history; and, like wars and preparations for wars, the productive system becomes always more efficient *and* always more wasteful and destructive. This is so even setting aside for the moment the considerable contribution capitalism has always made to the outbreak of war. Capitalism has done this through its intrinsic competition and conflicts for markets, resources, investment outlets, strategic locations and, in this century, in its military and paramilitary attempts to prevent, stifle, and subvert revolution over the globe.

In the period of capitalist history, it would be hard to say whether peace interrupts war or vice versa. Even in the bloody twentieth century, there may have been more waste, if less destruction, in the periods of peace than in those of war[3] because of the systematic, ubiquitous, and persistent restriction of production in agriculture and industry, or the waste of labor and materials and equipment in the promotion, packaging, and selling of commodities, or the pervasive practices of "deliberate obsolescence" in durable consumer goods, or the enormous amount of unused capacity and unemployed and underemployed labor that has characterized the entirety of this century (more than just "waste" to the unemployed, of course), or, to bring the catalog to an abrupt halt at its most wasteful activity, global "peacetime" military production and practices.

In all these and other ways, to degrees unimagined even by otherwise well-informed people, capitalist economies everywhere, with the United States always much in the lead, have become increasingly ingenious at finding means to use resources wastefully or not to use them at all. Meanwhile, the populace is told with increasing frequency and vehemence of actual or impending terrible scarcities (most especially of oil, the resource in scandalously excess supply in the late 1980s, as has been true for most of this century). What is the purpose of this seemingly insane "economics"? To maintain market stability and profitability and to maintain social peace, that is, to maintain existing national and international structures of profit and business and national power.[4]

A Litany of Waste

Because the notion of waste implies an opposed notion of usefulness, it is of course impossible to settle upon a definition that would find universal agreement. Like most others who have explored this dimension of economic life, I have adopted a notion of waste meant to understate deliberately the probable realities. Even so, the quantitative figures are staggering in themselves and extraordinary in their qualitative implications. For present purposes, I have accepted the conclusion that "useful output in the U.S. ecomony could have been $1.2 trillion higher in 1980 than it actually was . . . ; 49.6% higher than its 1980 level." Among other reasons for viewing this as a conservative understatement is its authors' counting about 70 percent of military output as "useful."[5]

To say that "capitalism has been simultaneously the most efficient *and* the most wasteful productive system in history" is to point to the contrast between the great efficiency with which a particular modern factory produces and packages a product, such as toothpaste, and the contrived and massive inefficiency of an economic system that has people pay for toothpaste a price over 90 percent of which is owed to the marketing, not to the production, of the dentifrice. So toothpaste is unimportant. Automobiles are not. Until recently, in the United States it was assumed that over 15 percent of all jobs were directly or indirectly connected with the production and use of the automobile: As autos went, so went the U.S. (and much of the world) economy. In a Federal Trade Commission inquiry in 1939, General Motors (GM) presented figures showing that a Chevrolet with a market price of $950 had production costs of about $150: The rest was for advertising, distribution, and profits (and the production costs of course included the trivial appearance changes that, it has been estimated, amount to at least one-third of production costs over time). To this it may be added that between 1928 and 1939, years encompassing the worst depression in history, profits for GM averaged a 35 percent return to net worth.[6] It should be noted that in 1939 the sales effort industry was only just beginning to master the art of waste. What is true for toothpaste and automobiles is true for almost all consumer goods and, surprisingly, a small but rising percentage of capital goods (for example, computers of one sort and another): The processes within which they are made and sold become always more efficient and, at the same time, always more costly to the society.

The foregoing is suggestive of a much broader and deeper process of waste. It is so broad and deep and its various elements so thoroughly mixed together—some of them obvious and others subtle—that here I can do little more than paint in sweeping brush strokes the main elements of the process. This will be done by an examination of three (artificially separated) "sectors": industry, the military, and agriculture, with their various means and areas of waste—with the understanding that there is considerable overlap in all respects. After that a closely connected but analytically separable (and increasingly desperate) problem will be explored, that of "destructive wastes," the wastes that contaminate the environment and poison or threaten the life process.[7]

Waste in Industry

At the center of the structure of waste in the industrial sector is "the sales effort." That comprises advertising, sales promotion, trivial product change, and finally, the shaping of social mentality. As Paul Baran put it several decades ago, "people steeped in the culture of monopoly capitalism do not want what they need, and do not need what they want."[8] U.S. society badly *needs* better health, housing, education, and transportation, for example; the people very much *want* more and newer autos, TVs, fast food, artificial stimulants, and so forth; and the public accepts (many people, with enthusiasm) extraordinary military expenditures at the same time as it accepts policies that have reduced the provision of what is needed and that have very much worsened the lives of about half the population of the United States.[9]

That such processes go on and accelerate is not due to a law of nature but to the power and the needs of those who possess economic and political strength. As I have noted more than once in earlier pages, the astounding productive capacities of the modern economy must find ways of maintaining profitability that leave undisturbed the main in-

stitutions of capitalism. The ways developed have been those of consumerism and militarization: Both of them have depended upon a
successful process of mind management, whatever else has been necessary.
Advertising *is* mind management, whether it be innocent or ominous,
for selling products or politics. And it is costly in money, resources, and
skills.

In 1983, U.S. business spent $75 billion on advertising; pharmaceutical
firms (mostly aspirin and stomach and nose soothers) alone spent $575
million. "Companies devoted 2 percent of the GNP in 1980 to advertising
expenditures. If they had spent as little—in real dollars per capita—as
they did in 1948, we would have saved . . . 1.2 percent of actual GNP."[10]
But of course this is only one part of the quantitative story and says
nothing about its larger meaning. The rest of the numbers would point
to the foolishness and uselessness of the product styling and change
that was being advertised, among other matters. Some of the other
matters are more important.

As only one instance among the more important matters, for example,
I might single out the poisoning of food. In the past few decades the
food industry has been completely revolutionized, in terms of its scope
(from largely local to national and eventually multinational), its products
(from largely natural to largely processed), and the degree to which all
foods are in small or large degree dependent upon additives, few of
them entirely safe, some of them very dangerous to health (such as
cyclamates and nitrates). Although much more than advertising has been
part of this evolution, it could not have taken place without advertising
and its various ramifications. In sum, advertising, costly as it may be
in dollars, labor, and materials, has its larger costs hidden in the processes
that are at its heart: the reshaping and the creation of needs for the
purposes of profit, irrespective of the consequences to society, nature,
and people.

To say, as I did above, that the sales effort is at the center of the
structure of waste is accurate. But that must be followed by saying that
the sales effort is part of industrial waste: the restricted use of industrial
equipment and labor, along with much of *what* is produced, and how
labor is used.

First, output restriction (that is, producing at less than optimal rates
of utilization, which tend to average around 85 percent in manufacturing,
for example) is a practice that can only take place to the degree that
an industry is noncompetitive in structure. Output restriction takes place
as an attempt to keep price from falling (or to support its increase),
and the practice cannot work unless the entire industry follows suit. In
a competitively structured activity like wheat farming, the natural tendency of the farmer when faced with falling prices is to *increase* production

to maintain income. And the consequence, because all farmers are naturally impelled to the same thing, is to increase supply and push price down even further. In order to prevent that, the effective tendency in most of agriculture since the 1920s has been that of government intervention and output quotas, along with supported prices. In almost all industries— autos, soap, cigarettes, beer, steel, aluminum, and so on—there are few enough sellers and a very few dominant sellers, so that there can be agreement. Because such agreements go against the antitrust laws, they are secret, tacit, hidden. But there is agreement, or, it may be insisted, extraordinary coincidence, year after year, in industry after industry.[11]

The world has been treated to frequent lessons about this since the oil crisis of the 1970s. It now knows that OPEC (and others) maintain prices by agreed upon output quotas and that when those quotas are violated, oil supplies increase and prices decline. That this is equally true for auto production, and almost everything else in modern industry, perhaps may not have been learned, but the facts are the same, if in different dress. When the average rate of use of manufacturing productive capacity is between 75 and 80 percent, as was true in the early 1980s, for example, there are of course many things involved. But if prices stay the same or rise as productive capacity is being underused, it is certain that collusive output restriction is at work. In some sense, it almost always is. That is, we may assume that, on the average, industrial output could be at least 5 percent higher than it is, were "spoiling the market" not a continuing fear. That is a lot of waste, even if the foregoing estimates are high by a factor of two.

The waste in what is produced is perhaps easier to see. So much of what is produced is designed not to last beyond a certain length of time, whose reasonableness is a function, not of engineering or physical criteria, but of demand and market saturation. If the auto industry, to use its capacity profitably, must have an average buyer hold on to a new car for three years and then buy another new one, then it becomes auto *industry* practice to build cars that, after three years, begin to run up substantial repair bills (while advertising and model changes are building desire). And given the structure of income distribution, there will always be those who find those three-year-old cars better buys than holding on to their six-year-old cars. What is more, the car makers make a goodly share of their profits from the sale of parts.

Not every industry can come close to the auto industry in these respects, but planned obsolescence is the rule, whether by means of product failure, fashion, or some other method of assuring that products will not last longer than a well-priced market can bear. The ultimate in this, a growing phenomenon of the past decade or so, is the "use and throw away" product, normally made of plastic (therefore, more products are being made of plastic—which falls into the area of destructive wastes). None of the foregoing has any reference to the production of commodities created for the "man—or woman or child—who has everything," though it is likely that if this productive capacity were used less wastefully, it could make a significant contribution.

Let us turn instead to the enormous and increasing waste of human energy and skills, the waste of labor in industry. That waste may be measured in many ways: (1) unemployment and underemployment, (2) the productive efficiency of those who work full-time, and (3) the allocation of labor between productive and nonproductive jobs.

Unemployment and Underemployment. In the recession of 1956–1957, a full-page ad in the *Wall Street Journal* asked: "What's Wrong with a Little Recession?" Not much, it went on to answer, in that it loosens up the labor market and reduces inflationary threats. Those who hire labor, like those who buy products, like supply to exceed demand. In relation to labor, that means when there are more workers than jobs, when there are unemployed and underemployed workers. It is both interesting and ominous that the generally agreed upon (by academics and government) definition of "full employment" is now 6 percent unemployed; in the 1960s, it was 3 percent. Not that anyone believes that 6 percent equals zero (or that 3 percent did), but when there is less unemployment than the defined level, there is also trouble—for employers and for prices. Like the matter of output restriction, this particular view is an implicit confirmation of monopolistic structures in the economy. Although it is true that falling unemployment means higher wage pressures for employers, whether monopolistic or competitive, it will only mean higher prices (rather than lower profits) if the employers can pass their cost increases on in the form of price increases.

In any case, unemployment in the United States in the years since 1900 (excluding the years of World Wars I and II) has averaged 6.9 percent. And this says nothing about those who, working half-time or less, wish to work full-time or those who are trained steelworkers but work in jobs requiring few or no skills. It also says nothing about those who, because they have unsuccessfully sought jobs for so long that they have ceased to try—the "hard-core unemployed"—are not officially unemployed, for one is not considered unemployed unless one is known to be seeking work without finding it. One is not in the labor force otherwise. It is estimated that a figure for the rate of unemployment that included all these would be at least 50 percent higher than the official rate.[12]

That the level of employment and unemployment is not set by social laws but by the structures of social power is revealed when such rates are compared among capitalist countries. Between 1961 and 1980, the average annual unemployment rate in the United States was 5.7 percent; in capitalist Germany it was 1.4 percent, and it was 1.9 percent in Sweden. In the latter two countries, the politics and strength of labor and socialist movements have, in conjunction with governing coalitions, "consistently pursued policies which aim to smooth the cyclical fluctuations of market economies, providing cushions for those who feel the sharpest jolts and reducing the inflationary pressures which full employment policies can sometimes generate."[13] It is worth pondering how much more could have been produced with all that unused labor in this century (and the unused capacity, as well). One could come up with a number however arbitrary, for that; one could not come up with a number for the qualitative side of all this unused and underutilized labor, for the education and training and morale that could have been had there been a society seeking to use and develop, rather than simply to use, its human resources.

The Productive Efficiency of Those Who Work Full-time. Anyone who has ever worked in a factory, an office, a store, even a hospital or a school, knows of the extensive and virtually systematic "soldiering on the job" that characterizes almost all jobs—"when the boss isn't looking." This is true despite all the supervisory personnel who are paid to "look." It is true for two major reasons: morale and fear. The fear comes from the widespread (and usually accurate) belief that working faster will mean working oneself out of a job: Insecurity about continuing employment is endemic for virtually all wageworkers. The morale problem relates to workers' commitment to their job, employer, and/or product. Workers are seldom treated as full human beings—in terms of rights, intelligence, feelings—on the job, and the less so when the enterprise is a giant one. Workers know that what they work with is designed to be foolproof and that they are the fools. And they know well before the consumer does if the product they are producing is shoddy, or ill designed, or designed to fall apart at some early time. Workers may or may not believe they are being exploited, but they know they are being used and that, like some of their products, they are destined for rapid discard. Only genuine fools would be able to maintain their morale under such conditions. Worker ownership and/or control (within the capitalist system) can do and has done much to lessen this widespread alienation. It has been practiced not only in somewhat socialist societies such as Chile (before Augusto Pinochet) and Yugoslavia but also in many hundreds of firms in the United States. As things stand in the late 1980s, it is unlikely to spread; but things of all sorts are quite unlikely to stand as they are, as the crisis worsens. Meanwhile, worker discontent is another form of waste and one with rising effects in the social and political realm.[14]

The Allocation of Labor Between Productive and Nonproductive Jobs. Here I consider productive labor to be that which is working to produce goods and nonproductive labor as that which supervises and manages the former: managers and clerical and blue-collar supervisors. In the United States in 1980, such personnel constituted 10.8 percent of total nonagricultural employment. The figure for Sweden was 2.4 percent, for Germany 3.0 percent, and for Japan 4.4 percent. It would be difficult, and incorrect, to argue that the U.S. economy grew more rapidly than those did around 1980, that its productive efficiency was higher, or that its economy—or its worker morale—was healthier. If no justification can be found, perhaps an explanation can be. It connects with the arguments made in Chapter 2 on the rise of corporate (and governmental) bureaucracies. These grew in the period of U.S. dominance and then became, in keeping with Parkinson's Law, self-generating: "internal imperialisms." They are a large waste of human energy and talent. Considering that a high percentage of new jobs are in this area, finance, real estate, "paper pushing," the waste is even greater.

Military Waste

When one examines industry and agriculture for waste, whether in what is done or what is withheld, one locates certain areas of waste in what is generally (at least by present standards of useful production) *not* waste. The reverse is true in the realm of military production. The reference here is not to screwdrivers or toilet seats that should have been made in gold, considering the price that the Pentagon (that is, U.S. citizens) paid. Those are mere symbols, although telling ones, of an immense and scandalous and shocking reality, a reality constructed by the military, the main corporate beneficiaries, a long-standing and crowded assemblage of petty and great politicos, and a population all too willing to be made fools of, on the mistaken notion that such economic misdeeds are necessary for their jobs to go on. Their ethic is waste, and want not.

What is the reality? It is entirely too complex to be dealt with adequately here, but one can at least go beyond petty and amusing symbols. Part of the reality is found in numbers (dollars, for example), part of it in processes (planned obsolesence as high art, cost-plus pricing), part of it in economic and social consequences. I begin with some numbers.

I cannot refrain from also pointing to the word *military*. Almost everyone refers to military spending as *defense* spending: it certainly sounds more necessary, even useful. And it connects with an important terminological change in 1947. In that year, the year in which so much of what has determined the world's destiny was set rolling, the Department of War, as it had been called since the birth of the nation, was renamed the Department of Defense. This was done by the very people and at much the same time that the Central Intelligence Agency (CIA) was being constructed, along with the National Security Council. The draft, or selective service, was reinstituted that year by the very people who saw the defense of the United States as having to take place anywhere and everywhere in the world where developments displeasing to the United States might be taking place (or even *might* take place). The War Department fought very few wars; for the Defense Department, there may not have been a twelve-month period when it was not overseeing a war somewhere—declared or not, acknowledged or not.

So be it. But even if the United States does spend a lot, it spends only a small fraction of its GNP on the military, right? Wrong. Like so much else in contemporary government, what numbers are is determined by definitions. Thus, for example, as the Vietnam War heated up in dollars and blood, President Johnson, in addition to lying to his Bureau of Budget about its costs, also had instituted a change in the role of Social Security in the government's budget. Social Security is paid for by contributions, and benefits come from those contributions. It is self-supporting. Johnson had Social Security put into the budget, so that its income was seen as taxes and its benefits as expenditures. In doing this, he was enlarging the total amount of government expenditures considerably (without changing anything else) and thereby reducing the percentage of military expenditures to total government expenditures.[15]

But there is more to the numbers game than that. What the military costs is not measured by what the government spends on what are called defense expenditures. It should include also veterans' benefits, at least half the interest on the national debt (from past wars), the weapons portion of the Department of Energy budget, some forms of military assistance, a considerable, if not the entire, amount of space expenditures, and at least some portion of the CIA budget, the United States Information Agency budget, and a large percentage of foreign aid, in whatever name it passes.[16] Viewed in this light (apart from the Social Security change) military expenditures regularly exceed 50 percent of the federal government budget. The public is told, instead, that they are less than 10 percent of GNP and, at the most (under Reagan), something like 25 percent of federal expenditures. And what have they totaled over the years from 1946 on? Using the government's conservative definition of "national defense expenditures" as they appear in the annual President's *Economic Report*, the number comes in just under $4 *trillion*, through 1987. Moreover, the official percentage of GNP is just about half of what those expenditures mean to the capital goods industries, the heart of the industrial sector.[17]

The waste in the midst of all that is mind-boggling, and it takes various forms. *Item:* The antiballistic missile (ABM) missile complex in North Dakota cost $6 billion. It was completed in 1975. It was closed (for good) forty-eight days later. *Item:* It is in the very nature of military production that it is either used or not used. When used, it is consumed rapidly; mostly it is not used (for which, praise the Lord!). When not used, it is deliberately rendered obsolete by arms manufacturers (or, less frequently, by foreign developments). *Item:* Whether used or not used, it is produced almost entirely within "cost-plus" (that is, profit-guaranteed) contracts. Average final cost overruns average 320 percent of the winning estimate originally submitted (and if the costs are over three times greater, so are the profits: a rather small, indeed a reverse, incentive for efficient production, one might think). Nor do companies lose their privileged status if what they have produced and sold does not work according to promises or specifications; if they did, the military-industrial complex would be riddled by bankrupt companies.[18] *Item:* Among the many other possible instances, let us close with a question. Can anyone who has ever been in the army give an estimate of how much time is spent doing nonwork, or no work?

So granted all this, the reasonably well-informed working person says: It creates jobs, doesn't it? There the answer is in parts: (1) It certainly took us out of the depression, and because the needed level of government expenditures (military and nonmilitary) to prevent a serious recession/depression would not have been politically feasible without all those military expenditures, then the answer is "yes," but only up until, at best, the late 1960s. (2) At that time, some academic studies, some congressional studies (doubtless given their life by representatives dubious about the Vietnam War), and one trade union study (the machinists' union) all pointed in the same direction: If the level of government expenditures were to remain the same and if military expenditures were replaced by expenditures on schools, housing, education, and the like, the jobs per government dollar would be anywhere from one-third to over 50 percent higher. As time goes on that percentage rises, for the reason that is true in general; namely, since the 1960s the kinds of things that are meant by military expenditures are increasingly high-tech. A few hundred B-52s dropped more bombs on Vietnam than many many thousands of bombers did during World War II; one hydrogen bomb could itself outdo all of those; a nuclear submarine carries enough firepower on it to destroy many cities on one mission; and so on. These are all very high-tech products. A few of the largest corporations produce them, using relatively few highly trained workers (technicians and engineers). They all do well, but they are a small percentage of those who worked at River Rouge (the World War II B-24 plant of Ford Motor Company). In 1941, President Franklin Roosevelt asked for "50,000 planes" and helped to end the Great Depression. Reagan asked for $1.6 trillion to be spent in five years (and pretty much got it) and may be helping to bring a depression on.[19]

The statement that "a few" of the very largest corporations get most of the military contracts should perhaps be made more precise. In so doing one should raise the implicit question as to why, if so few companies receive so many hundreds of billions of government dollars, decade after decade (for the figures and the companies are much the same going back to World War II) and perform the job so inefficiently (and with such great profits), why should all this be done by *private* companies? One hundred corporations regularly receive about two-thirds of all prime contracts (parts of which they then subcontract, increasing their already great power); the top thirty-three receive 50 percent; almost all of this is awarded within five industries: aircraft, electronics and telecommunications, shipbuilding and repairing, vehicles, and oil; about 90 percent of prime contracts are negotiated rather than won through competitive bidding (the latter is the exception, though it is supposed to be the rule); and, unsurprisingly, the profit rates of the top ten military contractors (in 1984) were 25 percent, twice that of manufacturing corporations in general that year.[20]

Finally, let us look at a contrast between the meanings of military and of social expenditures for the distribution of income. The high-tech that greatly and increasingly characterizes military production (which means that half as many wage earners but 20 percent more outlay in salaries result from a given dollar of government expenditure, compared with the average "social expenditure") has the effect of increasing the inequality of income distribution: All pay taxes, but those on the top receive disproportionate job benefits (to say nothing of corporate profits) from the military dollar. Not much of a surprise there, either.

"So," Michael Reich concluded, "military spending is easily expandable, is highly profitable, and benefits the major corporations in the economy."[21] And what the major corporations want, by and large, they get, at least more so than any other group.

Waste in Agriculture

Because agriculture means food and because there are so many hundreds of millions of people with terribly inadequate diets, waste in agriculture takes on an extra dimension. People's lives are made more difficult when auto production is restricted to maintain already monopolistically high prices or when petroleum-based products shoot up in price because of output-reducing agreements (which also immediately affect agriculture, increasingly dependent upon petrochemicals). But when, as in agriculture, there is a virtually permanent pattern of systematically *not* planting countless acres of previously and/or potentially cultivable lands, in all the major agricultural areas, for all the major crops, decade after decade; and when to that is added stored (and rotting) foodstuffs and destroyed crops, and so on ad nauseum, the problem is transformed from "only" consumer exploitation and (as in the case of oil) economic disturbance and waste into economic criminality. The system is responsible for avoidable mass malnutrition and brain damage (as well as outright starvation for at least ten million people a year), stunted lives and premature deaths for who knows how many millions of people on every continent, the annual deaths of hundreds of thousands of children from malnutrition-connected diarrhea, and intermittent famines. No continent is innocent of these horrendous crimes; and they worsen and spread as the spectacularly productive twentieth century lurches, or marches, to its end.

To insert social madness into what is already a nightmare, numberless peasants in Africa, Asia, and Latin America who in the recent or distant past managed to find a subsistence or better living from the lands they cultivated (inefficiently, no doubt) and (often) controlled have been displaced by giant (usually foreign) companies and modern techniques, not least in the name of "the green revolution." These people now wander or huddle in the countryside or clog the brutal cities, while constituting an always more abundant, always more desperate labor supply, willing to do almost anything for almost nothing. They eat much less than before, their social existence has been destroyed for profit, and they will not be rescued by any number of rock concerts.

Meanwhile, the heightened productivity and production of their former (and other) lands require even greater restrictions of production and more stored and rotting crops and products in other agricultural areas. All this is organized and supported by governments in all the major and minor nations, under increasing pressures from the small and even more from the corporate "farmer," all holding back food production in a starving and ill-fed world, all to keep prices and profits up, all in the name of the family farm (in the United States) or some idyllic unit that in any case disappears as the policies multiply, all in the name of social betterment.[22]

To the degree that agriculture has ceased to be "farming" and has become "agribusiness," that is, characterized by corporate ownership, often diversified into other, nonagricultural businesses, the restricted and wasteful production in agriculture has the same roots and the same obstacles to beneficial change as wasteful production in industry. But to the considerable degree that small farmers remain in agriculture—more considerable as a percentage in Japan and Western Europe (including Britain) than in the United States—there is an important difference. Farmers want to farm—profitably, to be sure. Farmers, as distinct from the agricultural corporation, would very much prefer producing as much as possible on their lands and live up to their self-image as providers of lifestuffs; farmers have always felt uncomfortable with output-restricting policies. In this world, farmers use their political clout (which is notable in Japan and Western Europe) to keep prices up and supplies down. But one may hope that they would be political allies in the kinds of output-increasing policies to be proposed in the next chapter.

Mother Nature in the Gunsight:
Destructive Wastes

Human beings are, of course, one part of nature, along with other animals, the seas, the forests, the land. But humans are the only part of nature that can change, and change irreversibly, the rest of nature, and in doing so, they change themselves, for better or for worse. Earthquakes destroy, as do floods; beavers chew down trees and dam up creeks; lightning sets forests on fire. But the damage done in these and all other instances of natural alteration is soon absorbed or reversed; in any case, they are local matters.

Not so for humans. In being the most creative and constructive of nature's elements, people are at the same time the most careless and destructive—careless of their well-being and destructive of their environment and, through wars (and other violence), their fellow human beings. Even more, as is now a commonplace, people are moving toward transformations of nature so substantial (not including nuclear warfare) as to be irreversible and damaging on what is still an unimaginable scale. (The reference is to the ozone layer, the warming of the earth, and other such global disruptions of nature.) *Item:* As the forests of the Amazon Basin disappear, in consequence of an accelerating and spreading exploitation (for profit, of course), so do the oxygen supply and the bird population of the Northern Hemisphere disappear, proportionately. These disappearances are connected with each other and are also connected with the larger processes of economic and social recklessness that characterize the world in this century—at always-accelerating rates, despite the warnings of the worldwide scientific community.

How does all that connect with the capitalist process? Is it not merely an outcome of otherwise benign industrialism, a set of processes one neither wishes to nor has the ability to alter substantially? In this compact discussion, as earlier regarding other complex matters, I cannot do more than point to some of the basics; for present purposes, that must suffice. As for capitalism, let us begin at the heart of the matter: expansion. Throughout capitalist history, economic expansion (accumulation) has been like an all-powerful magnet pulling the economic process ever faster through time and space; it, and the profit seeking (and need) that energizes the capitalist process, have always been and remain heedless of the consequences to all but "the bottom line." Indeed, Milton Friedman, probably the most effective ideologue of "market capitalism" in the past several decades, insisted that the capitalist himself has a duty *not* to think of anything but profits (and that which supports them, which does not include Mother Nature) and the society a duty *not* to interfere with the capitalist—a parody of Adam Smith, but much listened to these days. (Friedman also believes that *everything* should be privately owned and operated for profit: jails, schools, parks, the military, hospitals, and . . . everything. And recently, especially in the United States and Great Britain, the process has been going his way.)

Until one thinks about it, it sounds like a good idea. When one thinks about it, one discovers that although the capitalist takes the gain from this process, everyone else, including by now Mother Nature, pays the costs. When economists first began to think about such matters, they used the term *external diseconomies*. But what they had in mind was minimal compared to the natural disasters the public now lives with, to say nothing of those that are just over the horizon. And even at their best, such economists did not realize that as corporate power grew, and as it became conscious of both profit possibilities from the status quo and the threat of alternatives environmentally less dangerous, the corporations would use their immense economic *and* political power to "counter, suppress, and eliminate" those other possibilities.[23]

Let us return to the fundamental structures and processes of the contemporary capitalist system. The need for substantial economic expansion has, as productive capacities have grown so greatly in this century, produced the need to waste (within the framework of capitalist views). The same processes that have created all the waste already discussed have produced the destructive wastes with which we are now concerned. It is not that wastefulness and destructive wastes began to occur first in the twentieth century; it is rather that their amounts and their types taken together have made what was at most a passing problem, formerly, into a major threat. For example, if an industrial plant dumps chemical wastes into a large river at the rate of X units/day, the river can cleanse itself. If ten more plants on the same river do the same, the problem is altered. If both banks of the river become dotted with such plants and if their effluents are of a higher form of toxicity, the river will be destroyed, and what has depended upon it (people, for drinking; agriculture, for irrigation) then finds itself faced with major problems. As the rate and spread of economic expansion and industrialization have grown in this century, this process of natural destruction has become ubiquitous, in the air, the water (bays, rivers, lakes, even oceans), and the soil, and in turn has of course found its way into food chains on the land and in the seas.

In a rich country like the United States (I shall note important differences for Tier III countries in Chapter 5), there is no need for further growth in real gross national product. What *is* needed is a substantial change in the composition of production, in what is produced and in what relative quantities. To put it simply for the moment, we need fewer guns and more butter, fewer autos and more public transportation, fewer financial services and more health services. For the capitalist system it is quantitative increase rather than qualitative improvement that is vital; for the population, it is the reverse if they are to have quantitative improvement along with better lives. For the Tier III countries (as well as some of those in between Tiers II and III, such as Brazil or Portugal) the kinds of badly needed quantitative increases cannot occur without qualitative changes within their own societies and changed relationships in the world economy (as will be discussed later).

Here it will behoove us to pin down some of the gloomy pronouncements made above. This shall be done with respect to three important and closely connected areas: transportation, energy, and petrochemicals, by no means the entirety of what is here relevant.

Transportation

Few would disagree with the notion that the definition of a good transportation system would stress safety, convenience, comfort, speed, and the efficient use of resources. A transportation engineer asked to design a system to meet such standards in engineering rather than profit terms (after distinguishing between cargo and passengers) would have us fly very long distances, go by rail between city and suburb and between cities only two or three hundred miles apart, use public transportation systems within cities (underground and surface rail systems, electrified), and private (or rented) automobiles for recreational and some few other purposes. Such a system would be safer, more convenient, more comfortable, faster, and more efficient of resources in extraordinary degree by comparison with (most particularly in the United States) what is increasingly done: going by private car everywhere, every day, except when flying (and then driving to the airport). Cargo is carried in almost as foolish a pattern, using trucks (and even when there is no hurry, air) instead of rail. All of this is true despite the well-known facts of the matter. For example:

- To go from Boston to New York City requires ten gallons of gasoline per person by air, seven by private auto, and two by rail (assuming each vehicle to be half full).
- The dependence upon the private auto instead of mass urban transit causes 50 percent more fuel to be consumed.
- It takes six times as much fuel to haul a ton of freight from Los Angeles to New York by truck than by train.[24]

In addition to using more oil and gasoline, current practices also pollute the air more than the alternative would. They are also more profitable to the petroleum and automobile corporations, among other giant businesses (and relatively smaller ones, such as motels).

This dangerous and wasteful system of transportation not only did not just "happen"; it required the undoing of a more sensible system that had preceded it. Thus, by way of example, when the San Francisco Bay Bridge was completed and opened in 1939, its upper deck had five lanes for autos, and its lower deck was divided between a two-way truck road and an electric railway system. By the early 1950s, both decks were being used for cars, buses, and trucks, and the clean, swift, safe, and cheap electric trains had disappeared. The public was never consulted; indeed, when the public began to understand what was happening, too late, it tried to stop it. What had happened?

General Motors, in conjunction with Standard Oil of California and the Firestone Tire Company, through their holding company, National City Lines, purchased the transbay Key System, subsequently dismantled the train system and put buses in its place (General Motors is the largest diesel bus manufacturer). Subsequently, the bus system was sold to a local company with the stipulation that the purchase of new equipment "using any fuel or means of propulsion other than gas[oline]" was strictly prohibited. The inadequacies of this system were an important factor in causing an increase in the sale and use of cars to move across the San Francisco Bay. Today crossing the bridge for commuters means endless traffic jams, great expense, and no little danger. What was done there and then occurred in dozens of other urban areas in sixteen different states. In doing these things, General Motors and its partners were not acting illegally; it made good business sense for auto, gas, and rubber manufacturers to take steps to build their market and let the devil take the hindmost.[25]

Next to military expenditures, the least controversial form of government expenditures has been that on highways. From the late 1940s, highway expenditures became a steady outlet for federal and state moneys and, like the military counterpart, were very popular with businesses (construction, equipment, metals, oil, truckers, motels) and labor, as a means of maintaining or increasing profits and jobs. In fact such allocations were virtually unbeatable in the political realm. However, as Michael Best and William Connolly wrote, "it was disastrous for the country. Besides the strain it imposes on our fuel resources, it has created cities crisscrossed with highways, straddled by distorted housing patterns, smothered in toxic emissions of carbon monoxide, lead, and other deadly chemical combinations."[26]

It has been emphasized throughout this book that economic expansion is the highest standard of economic conduct; it also serves to place noneconomic standards in a secondary position, when appropriate. Thus, because of the growing recognition since the 1950s of the dangers of the always more polluted air, by the late 1960s legislation was developed to control, among other things, auto emissions; by the early 1970s such laws were pretty well in place. The automobile companies had strongly but unsuccessfully tried to prevent this (as they have done with other safety matters). But when, in 1975–1976, there was a serious recession, hitting the automobile industry with the greatest severity, the laws were suspended, quite consciously placing growth before safety, with barely a peep of protest.

Energy

The wastefulness and dangers of the transportation system are in some sense the Siamese twin of the same problems in the energy system, although the latter includes others as well, especially connected with nuclear energy production and wastes. The most powerful companies in the world today are energy companies: "energy," not oil, or gas, or coal. The largest energy companies of the late 1980s are owned and controlled by the major oil companies. The latter are also the major natural gas, coal, and uranium companies—already, or almost. They began to be so well before the oil crisis of the 1970s; with that crisis, long-term tendencies were accelerated. Consequently, no matter *what* happens that might cause a shortage or price increase for any source of energy, it is beneficial to the major energy companies (the most major of which, of course, is Exxon). It is not difficult to believe that they cooperated with more than resisted the OPEC price increases after 1973: As in GM buying up urban mass transit systems, "it makes sense."

The waste in the energy industry is fabled. The pattern of land ownership and use in the United States has led to "competitive drilling" for crude oil, as compared with the "unit field" system in Saudi Arabia, for example. What might cost $15 a barrel to extract in Texas costs perhaps $2 in the Middle East. More than that, this pattern of extraction means that about two-thirds of the oil is left in the ground or can be taken out only at even higher costs. (Instead of being blown out by pressure, it has to be pumped out.) Similarly, about half of underground coal is left in the mine. And none of this has reference to the wastes of distribution, conversion, and use. The public is told daily of the preciousness of energy supplies, and those who make these pronouncements participate actively in throwing those supplies to the winds.[27]

The wastes and the destructive wastes in petroleum and coal are substantial and always more frightening; one tends to forget them momentarily, however, when considering nuclear energy. Three-Mile Island, in Pennsylvania, and Chernobyl, in the USSR, both slowly fading into memory, were once abrupt reminders of just how dangerous nuclear power plants are and suggestive of how very much more dangerous they are likely to show themselves to be—when, where, how, is not yet known. The waste is manifold for such plants: They are so dangerous that many that have been built have never opened and never will; many are closed a good part of the time; some have been used and closed for good (in both senses of the term). Taken together they amount to hundreds of billions of dollars spent for danger and waste. (And no reference is here made to government nuclear plants for weapons use.)

Waste disposal is a major problem with many dimensions: chemical wastes, garbage, and most ominous by far, nuclear wastes. The odyssey of the New York City garbage-filled barge in its six-month quest (in 1987) for a resting place was pretty funny, but of course it stood for something not funny at all. There is nothing remotely funny about the disposal of chemical wastes, whether into waterways or holes—as the continuing Love Canal (New York State) story has revealed. And the problem of nuclear waste disposal is so forbidding that one can barely force oneself to think about it.

I am not referring to something that is merely potential. It is already an old problem, with origins in all the nuclear energy or products that have been produced, for homes or weapons, in the United States, or Britain, or France, or Sweden, or the Soviet Union, or China. The stuff goes on being dangerous for thousands of years, and the "bottom line" is that there is no safe place to put it, on land or in the sea. If, by some as yet unexplained process, the world manages to avoid more nuclear war (after Hiroshima and Nagasaki, that is), it seems quite possible that through the combination of unsafe plants and poisonous wastes humanity might well "nuke" itself quite substantially from sheer social carelessness. That same carelessness or, perhaps, recklessness is eating away at human lives, and what supports these lives, quietly, invisibly, increasingly. It does not make headlines, and is without the drama of Three-Mile Island and Chernobyl, but it is no less deadly for that.

Petrochemicals

Through every day and night, everyone in the leading industrial countries (and a growing percentage of all others) is eating something, wearing something, cleaning oneself or car or house with something, sleeping on something, surrounded by something made from oil: petrochemicals and their numberless products and offshoots. They have taken the place of something natural, or organic—cotton or wool, steel or copper or wood, animal wastes (for fertilizer)—or they are put into otherwise natural products to preserve them or make them more attractive (among other purposes), such as additives in foods and other products.

As one of several manifestations of the so-called chemical revolution of this century, this trend began in Germany when it developed coal tar derivatives (largely by I. G. Farben) for its explosives industry and as a substitute for its lack of key resources (including oil). That unpleasant beginning now has an unpleasant middle and threatens a considerably more unpleasant end. When Rachel Carson wrote *Silent Spring* (published in 1962), the silence she was concerned with was that of birds, which had disappeared. She sounded an early-warning alarm about the supercession of nature's life-long connections and mutual dependencies (such as between birds and insects) and how that would slowly but inexorably set up a chain of circumstances destroying, not supporting, life.

In the mid-1970s, a popular TV commercial in the United States had the theme: "You can't fool Mother Nature." With respect to synthetic products and petrochemicals in their manifold uses, there is a range of meanings that verify that homily. First, the evolution of the natural order, a matter of who knows how many billions of years, established for all living things various processes of life, from beginning through natural disappearance.

Nature cannot handle synthetics, chemically synthesized artificial products: detergents in the rivers, bays, and oceans quite simply never disappear; plastic containers do not rot, nor do those aluminum cans in their billions (which the public is at least learning to recycle in the millions); pesticides kill some insects, allow others to multiply, and at the same time poison the soil; synthetic fertilizers are at the very best questionable in their effects on food. In short, an as yet unknown, but surely high, percentage of these synthetic products is toxic, and virtually all of them are nonbiodegradable; that is, they must be carried away and be buried, or sunk, or something: thus that Homeric New York barge.

It is easy to believe that modern society has found this demon by reverse serendipity, that is, that an unstoppable technological process of undeniable goodness has somehow been found to be cancerous (as so many of those additives are in fact). But that is only a good cover story; the truth is that all these products are quite simply more profitable to produce and sell (and are produced and sold, almost always, by giant companies) than their natural or organic predecessors, even though they all are more dangerous, or at least more troublesome, to people and society.[28]

Already Bigger than a Man's Hand

If the lamentations that have run through this chapter had begun to be serious only just now and their origins and nature unknown until recently, that would be sufficient cause for alarm. But even more alarming is that none of this is new. Air and soil pollution, toxic substances in our food supply, the disappearance of resources (such as forests, waterways, animals), or the problem of nuclear wastes—all these matters have been known about from their onset. In some cases, it may be said that there has been criminality involved, for example, when asbestos companies deliberately hid from the workers their high probabilities of contracting and dying from asbestosis.[29]

The scientists who developed the atomic bomb knew from the first what the dangers of nuclear developments were, and the appropriate governmental and private agencies were always cognizant of the dangers. But the twin motivations of power and profit were sufficient to cause those agencies to conceal the truth, to falsify records, and to continue to do so. Much the same is so for all those concerned with all the dangerous products and practices, as it is also so that some significant share of corporate support for political candidates on the local, state, and national level is conditional upon their promised opposition to environmental protection and to safety and health standards for workers.

Consequently, along with the rising public awareness and development of governmental institutions to reverse the processes of natural and social damage, those processes continue to increase. Indeed, when, in the "good news," one is told of progress, it is never explained that the progress is limited to lowering the rate of *increase* of damages.[30]

What has brought the world to its current fearful environmental condition is what has also taken the world economy to crisis: the fundamental need and drive for expansion, the main ways and means by which expansion takes place, and the motives and power of those who direct the process. Or in different words, it is the ceaseless and voracious chase after profits and power, the adoption of any means to those goals irrespective of the human, natural, or social consequences of the means. Moreover, it is the direction of the private and public processes of life by supercorporations and the superstate, both substantially militarized in ideology and practice, that has taken the world there, while also discarding or crushing any alternative.

There have been and are alternatives. One flourished long ago in the geographic area of the United States, and it was extinguished brutally and with all possible speed. It was the civilization of those who preceded the Europeans in North America. The chief of a Native American tribe has left us this to ponder:

> As to us, we find all our riches and all our conveniences among ourselves, without troubles, without exposing our lives to the dangers in which you find yourselves constantly through your long voyages; and whilst feeling compassion for you in the sweetness of our repose, we wonder at the anxieties and cares which you give yourselves, night and day. . . . Now tell me this one little thing, if thou has any sense, which of these two is the wisest and happiest? He who labours without ceasing and only obtains with great trouble enough to live on, or he who rests in comfort and finds all he needs in the pleasures of hunting and fishing?[31]

The world cannot return, either economically or psychologically, to that condition of easy and natural balance, nor are there many who would choose to do so even were it possible. But we can seek to live at peace with our environment, at peace with our fellow human beings wherever they may be, and at peace also with ourselves in an urban and industrial world. We can, but not so long as the bulk of people in the United States and a rising percentage elsewhere continue to strive for a cornucopia of increasingly contrived and expensive consumer goods, led by those who strive for profits and power.

The time has come to take thought, to reflect on what are the genuine needs and pleasures of life, and to develop symmetry between ends and means. Those ends are not mysterious or the province of a few: to eat well, to be comfortably clothed and housed, to learn through education what one can do and be, to be healthy, to enjoy nature and human works, and to have control over one's life. But each of these ends moves farther away, not closer, with each passing year. Treasures are what one has been socialized to count as such though they defile one's life and tend to make people into robots: the automobile, the TV, the encapsulated suburban existence, the gleaming high buildings, the ever-rising (and always more useless) GNP, fast food. Human beings are moving in the wrong direction for themselves and for the rest of nature. To change, as Lincoln said in another context, "we must disenthrall ourselves." Some elements of what that might mean are presented in the next chapter.

Notes

1. The quoted phrase is from Lew Cawley's review of the film "Platoon," in *Monthly Review*, June 1987. It may be an oversimplification of the processes now to be discussed, but it is an evocative one.

2. R. H. Tawney, *Religion and the Rise of Capitalism* (New York: Mentor, 1950), p. 76.

3. The very notion of "periods of peace" raises important questions of definition and analysis, especially for a nation like the United States, whose announced and unannounced wars have always been fought elsewhere (in this century). Not only would most people in the United States see the present time as a period of peace, despite the definitive financing of the Contras in the Nicaraguan civil war (and some physical presence there and even more in Honduras), for example, but also most people in the United States in the 1950s thought of the years of the Korean War (officially classified as a United Nations "police action" in the United States) as such a peaceful period. With such confusions, the phrase may well lose its usefulness.

4. And what about these processes in the noncapitalist societies, such as the USSR, or China, or Cuba? Military expenditures are also substantial in *all* the noncapitalist countries, and inefficiency and waste are widespread. There are at least two points to be made for the purposes of my argument: (1) much of the military expenditures in the noncapitalist countries are a consequence of long years of "containment" and may reasonably be seen as defensive; in any case, they are never for purposes of using up excess productive capacity or maintaining profitability; and (2) apart from the ways in which these countries copy the capitalist countries in wasteful products (such as in auto design), their waste is due to weaknesses in their system; it is not a way to absorb the system's "unprofitable" strength. There is nothing directly for us to do with respect to countries outside the capitalist framework; this book is written for those inside.

5. Richard Edwards et al., *The Capitalist System* (Englewood Cliffs, N.J.: Prentice-Hall, 1986), p. 331. The other reasons include the fact that this estimate took no account of restricted production in industry or agriculture (such as underutilized equipment or acreage) or the waste in what is produced (e.g., in deliberately obsolete forms), or destroyed deliberately (e.g., coffee) or by rotting (as in grains and dairy products)—a large amount of waste. A considerable part of my Chapter 4 follows the lead, often word for word, of Chapter 9, "Waste and Irrationality," of this excellent collection of essays on various aspects of the system. In a generally strong book, Chapter 9 is one of the outstanding sections. The figures just cited were taken from the selection entitled "The Waste Economy," in turn excerpted from the important book by Samuel Bowles, David M. Gordon, and Thomas E. Weisskopf, *Beyond the Waste Land: A Democratic Alternative to*

Economic Decline (New York: Anchor Doubleday, 1983). Both for the next few pages in my Chapter 4 and again in Chapter 5, I have found this fine book most helpful. Still for this chapter, I have used other essays in Chapter 9 of *The Capitalist System* liberally—that by Michael Reich (written especially for the book), "The Irrational Attraction of Military Spending"; "The Source of Militarism," excerpted from Tom Riddell; "Militarism: The Other Side of Supply," from *Economic Forum,* Summer, 1982; and for my section on destructive wastes, "Nature and Its Largest Parasite," excerpted from the excellent book *The Politicized Economy,* by Michael H. Best and William E. Connolly (Lexington, Mass.: D. C. Heath, 1976). I may say that my pointed dependence on *The Capitalist System* is deliberate: It is an easily available book of great value, a book that interested readers may use to pursue all the issues raised in my book.

6. Federal Trade Commission, *Report on the Automotive Industry* (Washington, D.C.: U.S. Government Printing Office, 1940).

7. Pioneer analytical work regarding the socially wasteful processes of capitalism is put forth in K. William Kapp, *The Social Costs of Private Enterprise* (Cambridge: Harvard University Press, 1950), a work as widely neglected by the economics profession as it is deeply important. Barry Commoner was one of the first scientists to raise the alarm about environmental destruction, in *The Closing Circle* (New York: Alfred Knopf, 1971). For a more general and theoretical approach, see Edward N. Wolff, *Growth, Accumulation, and Unproductive Activity* (Cambridge: Cambridge University Press, 1987).

8. Paul A. Baran, *The Longer View* (New York: Monthly Review Press, 1969), p. 101. This is a collection of Baran's essays. Many of them, including the one in which the quoted statement appeared, were originally published in *Monthly Review,* in this case, in October 1959, in the essay "Marxism and Psychoanalysis."

9. One does not know where to begin or to end regarding human and social needs. It has been conservatively estimated that "approximately 50 million people still live in the deteriorated and socially dysfunctional areas called slums." This statement is found in the essay "Slums and Poverty," by Gary Knox, Chapter 9 of a most useful and relevant collection, *Social Costs in Modern Society,* edited by John E. Ullmann (Westport, Conn.: Quorum Books, 1983). In that same book, reference is made to S. Walter and P. Choate, *America in Ruins* (Washington, D.C.: Council of State Planning Agencies, 1981), and its estimate that the total bill for infrastructural (water systems, transportation, sewers, etc.) renewal would come to $3 trillion. And then came Reagan. That point was made on p. 227 in Ullman. (His book constitutes a rare recognition of K. William Kapp, cited earlier, and is dedicated to him and to Lore Kapp.)

10. Edwards et al., *Capitalist System,* p. 330.

11. For the dominance and practices of big business, see John M. Blair, *Economic Concentration: Structure, Behavior and Public Policy* (New York: Harcourt, Brace, Jovanovich, 1972). The author spent most of his professional life as a chief economist in the Federal Trade Commission. The extraordinary power of a relatively small number of corporations treated by Blair is a substantial understatement of the present situation. In the years since he wrote, and especially in the 1980s, the patterns of economic concentration have intensified. See also

Edward S. Herman, *Corporate Control, Corporate Power* (Cambridge: Cambridge University Press, 1981).

12. The costs of underemployment and unemployment must be counted in several ways: the loss of goods and services not produced, the loss of purchasing power that would stimulate the economy, and not least, the anxiety and demoralization of those who need and want more work. Estimates of the narrowest of these dimensions, lost purchasing power, are made by John Innes, in Chapter 7 of Ullman, *Social Costs*. Calculating conservatively for 1976, e.g., when the official unemployment rate was 7.7 percent, Innes placed the loss of purchasing power between $54 and $70 billion (pp. 114–118).

13. Edwards et al., *Capitalist System*, pp. 320–321. Many of the data preceding this quote are from the same pages.

14. See ibid., pp. 321–326, for a strong discussion of worker morale, control, and ownership. For a powerful analysis of just what and just how much the industrial worker has lost as the twentieth century has progressed, see Harry Braverman, *Labor and Monopoly Capital: The Degradation of Work in the 20th Century* (New York: Monthly Review Press, 1974). Also useful is Richard Edwards, *Contested Terrain* (New York: Basic Books, 1979), a careful analysis of the uses of business power in the workplace.

15. Hypothetically, if total government expenditures are $1 trillion and "national defense spending" is $300 billion, then the latter is 30 percent of government spending. If then Social Security, hitherto not a part of the budget, is added into both sides of the budget at, say $200 billion, military spending automatically decreases from 30 to 20 percent. Now you see it, now you don't.

16. Perhaps most important, the figures of military expenditure should be viewed in terms of what economists call "opportunity costs"—that is, what has been forgone in order that these expenditures might be made. There are at least two vital losses in this respect: (1) what could have been produced instead (assuming the same level of government spending) and (2) the higher number of jobs that would have been yielded for every dollar of government spending, had it been on nonmilitary rather than military goods and services. The data are impressive. Putting together work from various sources, John E. Ullman (in Chapter 15 of Ullman, *Social Costs*) showed, for example, that the cost of two B-1 bombers (seen as obsolete even before they became operational, incidentally) at $400 million equals the price tag for rebuilding Cleveland's water supply system; that the Navy's F-18 fighter program costs the same, $34 billion, as the amount it would take to modernize the U.S. machine-tool stock to bring it to the average level of Japan's; and so on. As for jobs, he showed that $1 billion spent on producing B-1 bombers, which generated 58,000 jobs, would generate 83,000 jobs if used for mass transit construction, 75,000 jobs in law enforcement, and, inter alia, 118,000 jobs in education. See pp. 230–242. (I discuss this further in the following pages.) Ullman's Chapter 15 opened with the words of President Eisenhower, uttered in 1953: "Every gun that is made, every warship launched, every rocket fired signifies in the final sense a theft from those who hunger and are not fed, those who are cold and not clothed. This world in arms is not spending money alone. It is spending the sweat of its laborers, the genius of its scientists, the hopes of its children" (p. 227).

17. See James Cypher, "Capitalist Planning and Military Expenditures," in *Review of Radical Political Economics* 6 (Fall 1974), and James O'Connor, *Fiscal Crisis of the State* (New York: St. Martin's Press, 1973), Chapter 4 and its Table 2, for a representative composition of the national budget.

18. Edwards et al., *Capitalist System*, p. 335. Reich showed that "of thirteen major aircraft and missile programs since 1955 which cost $40 billion, only four (costing $5 billion) performed at as much as 75% of the design specifications. Yet the companies with the poorest performance records reported the highest profits" (ibid.).

19. Ibid.

20. Ibid., pp. 334–335. In 1962 (the "high-tech" has gone much higher since) the Department of Labor showed that military-space-oriented electronic plants had about 60 percent "highly-paid engineers, executives, or skilled blue-collar craftsmen. In the consumer-oriented plants of the same industry, in contrast, 70.2% of the employees were semi-skilled and unskilled blue- and white-collar workers" (ibid., p. 338).

21. Ibid.

22. The following data reported by *U.S. News and World Report* (May 23, 1988) underscore the paradox that as world food production in the 1980s has increased (wheat production by 11.6 percent between 1982 and 1986, for example), hunger has become more widespread and calamitous. "Today, the world lies awash in surplus. In 1986, European storage facilities held beef stocks equal to nearly one third of the global meat trade; U.S. silos bulged with stock totaling two years' worth of world grain exports. . . . Worldwide demand for imported food, which quadrupled in the 1970s, is down 30 percent since 1980. The developed world now spends $150 billion a year subsidizing bumper crops. Every American, for instance, spends $126 a year supporting U.S. farm programs through higher taxes and heftier grocery prices." Farmers could produce as much as their acreage and technology would allow, sell at free market prices, and be free of income distress, and they would much prefer to do so. That this has been done, and how it can be done will be discussed in Chapter 5. The human costs of this economic folly were underscored by Frederick P. Gerken: "At a time (1982) when the Reagan administration was cutting 900,000 households off welfare rolls and reducing benefits to 70 percent of all food stamp recipients, $2.2 billion (was spent) . . . just to keep certain dairy products off the market; some 13.8 billion pounds of milk, about 10 percent of production, had to be bought by the government. Some $400 million must be spent on storage and interest on the money paid out for the 1 million tons of commodities that are involved." Gerken was cited in Chapter 13, "Food," of Ullman, *Social Costs*, p. 215. The U.S. Agriculture Department reported on May 19, 1988, that "U.S. farmers will leave 76 million acres of farmland unplanted this year," an amount of land equal in area to the entire states of Illinois and Iowa. This happens as "drought-like conditions" in the United States are causing commodity prices to rise "dramatically from year-ago levels." See *San Francisco Chronicle*, May 20, 1988. See also Edward Higbee, *Farms and Farmers in an Urban Age* (New York: Twentieth Century Fund, 1963), an old but not out-of-date study. That farmers

(especially small farmers) are not the prime beneficiaries of high food prices was well shown in Nick Eberstadt, "Myths of the Food Crisis," *New York Review of Books*, February 19, 1976. The "green revolution" is discussed historically and analytically in Bernhard Glaeser (ed.), *The Green Revolution Revisited: Critiques and Alternatives* (London: Allen and Unwin, 1987).

23. Edwards et al., *Capitalist System*, p. 350. The air is not polluted only over the United States (Japan is probably worse, for example) nor only in capitalist skies. Other forms of environmental damage also go beyond the capitalist world. The basic industrial system and the chase after economic expansion are ubiquitous, for historical reasons I shall not go into here.

24. Ibid., pp. 351–352.

25. Bradford Snell put together the research for a comprehensive historical study presented to the Senate Judiciary Subcommittee on Antitrust and Monopoly, available through the U.S. Government Printing Office as *American Ground Transport: A Proposal for Restructuring the Automobile, Truck, Bus, and Rail Industries*, U.S. Senate Document, 1972.

26. Edwards et al., *Capitalist System*, p. 353. This section on transport, energy, and petrochemicals has depended greatly on Best and Connolly, *Politicized Economy*, parts of which also appeared in *The Capitalist System*.

27. Edwards et al., *Capitalist System*, pp. 353–354. On oil company cooperation with OPEC, see Michael Tanzer, *The Energy Crisis* (New York: Monthly Review Press, 1974).

28. See Edwards et al., *Capitalist System*, for a discussion of petrochemicals and also of the industrial practices that endanger the health and lives of workers, pp. 355–357. Commoner, *The Closing Circle*, should be read to comprehend the full impact of contemporary industrial practices.

29. Johns-Manville, the principal asbestos products company in the world, for many decades hid the deadly truth from its working people and denied its causation as they fell ill and died. And when the facts finally became public and undeniable *and* litigated, the corporation split off its asbestos division, declared it bankrupt (with the friendly cooperation of the government), and if it succeeds in holding to that status, thereby deprived the dwindling number of survivors any financial relief. The wheels of justice do not even grind slowly in such matters.

30. Just as the definition of unemployment is intermittently changed to keep the official rate from rising in keeping with the facts (most recently, the Reagan administration altered the definition of the labor force to include the military, thus, as with Social Security and the military budget, inflating the base and lowering the percentage of unemployed), so does the definition of what constitutes *dangerous* levels of air pollution continue to rise as air pollution increases. It may be noted that it is quite possible to lower urban air pollution to tolerable levels by curbing industrial and private practices. In London, after more than 4,000 deaths were attributed to smog by the medical authorities, steps were taken that, though scarcely bringing back clean air, made the London air less deadly. Interestingly, it was also in London, more than a century earlier, that the powers-that-were, faced with rising numbers of dead from cholera (from

sewer gas and related developments) that did not single out only the poor, took the steps necessary to reduce that threat. Wisdom in the historical process is clearly not cumulative.

31. He was speaking to a French naval officer, in the early days of settlement of Europeans in North America. This, along with other useful materials, is to be found in Paul Jacobs, Saul Landau, and Eve Pell (eds.), *To Serve the Devil* (New York: Vintage, 1971), vol. 1, pp. 43–44. There are two volumes. Each volume contains a brief narrative history that introduces documents concerning the early history of the treatment in North America of Native Americans, African slaves, and people from Latin America and from Asia.

CHAPTER 5

New Directions

Introduction

Many, many changes within and between the participants in the world economy are needed and desirable; by no means are all of them even remotely possible in the foreseeable future. The framework within which appropriate policies may be developed must have several dimensions, responding to immediate, longer-run, and fundamental economic issues, as well as to the complex and bristling politics of this era, dominated as they have been by the cold war. And just as the United States took the lead in bringing the present capitalist system into existence, it must take the lead in steering it away from the abyss it now approaches. All these matters are intimately related, of course, and what follows will not seek to keep them entirely separated. Nor is it meant to be more than suggestive: What is intended below is to sketch out the main policy combinations that are necessary if any one of them is to succeed; to bring together economic with political, domestic with global, considerations; and to provide occasional references to the many books that have appeared recently proposing ways toward a safer and better world.

The global economic crisis moves toward two different forms of disaster—by explosion or by drowning. The explosive outcome would originate in a breakdown of the international financial system; the world economy is already sinking and may drown because of its inability to deal constructively with excess productive capacity. These two, excess capacity and financial fragility, are of course connected in origin, and they will be connected in their outcomes.

The always increasing, frenzied financial speculation in the late 1980s has many facets and causes, but its basis is to be found in the uneven or low profitability of the productive sector stemming from overcapacity (as was true in the 1920s). The increase of that overcapacity, moreover, has led to business and state policies (such as enormous military expenditures and deficits) that have promoted financial speculation and that make the financial system always more fragile. That occurs because the debtors in the world economy become weaker when they are faced with global excess capacity.[1]

Because of its inherently unstable tendencies, the dense network of connections of the various elements of the financial system, the great and growing importance of "hot money" (money tainted by illegality and money that moves so fast among the major banks that it heats up), and the links between all of these and the "instantizing" impact of electronic networks, the probability is greatest that the present crisis will move into disaster first through explosion and cause the already slowly sinking real economy to plunge to the bottom. This would be a replay of 1929 and then of the 1930s, with of course substantial variations for better and for worse.[2]

The world economy has moved into its condition of chronic weakness because of a complex dynamic that combines economic with political with military with social processes, structures, and attitudes, and again, national with international problems and institutions. Emergence from the crisis in any beneficial manner will also depend on such complexity, and on making appropriate changes in all the elements that dominate the social process. Faced with such a challenge, one would have to be foolish indeed to move ahead with high hopes. But one must try, most sensibly making the effort as Antonio Gramsci did, in Benito Mussolini's Italy: "Pessimism of the intellect, optimism of the will."[3] And hope for a better fate than his.

I shall begin with the international financial system and confront its two aspects that are most susceptible to relatively simple policy changes (where "simple" does not mean easy to effectuate): its high degree of instability and the global debt problem. It is impossible to prevent international financial collapse by changes in the international financial sector alone, as by now should be clear. For that reason and others, equally compelling, policies must be developed with respect to the real world of production, excess capacity, and waste, the real world of the cold war and its political economy, of desperate Tier III economies, of failing industrialism in (among other countries) the United States, and some combination of desperation and foolishness as well in agriculture and in the service sector. It will be argued that all these can be transformed from threat to possibility, especially (and probably only) if they are seen as part of an interdependent whole.

Financial Reforms

The financial system in the United States and in most other countries, as well as the global links that tie them together, is badly in need of a multiplicity of changes and needs them more every day, as the galloping impact of deregulation makes itself felt. Most of the regulations that affect contemporary banking have their origins in the years before World War II and even if retained would be inadequate to deal with the financial debacle. But the deregulation that began in the 1970s and then accelerated in the 1980s has had the effect of making a bad situation worse. The frauds and scandals that shook the banking and securities world in the United States in the 1920s were very much the consequence of a laissez-faire financial system, and subsequent reforms were an attempt to prevent their recurrence. But the ideology of political leaders today (not least in Britain and the United States) seems a satire, almost a caricature of that earlier period—and in an even more volatile, considerably more dangerous world situation. But as each piece of deregulation is accompanied by another financial shenanigan, the call for more deregulation is heard.[4]

That process will not be fully reversed in a short number of years; perhaps it cannot be reversed at all without the financial collapse it is likely to produce. But there are two areas of the financial world where immediate change is necessary and, perhaps, the least impossible. These two, and only these two, will now be explored. First, means must be developed to exercise control over the raging rivers of global finance, particularly in the Eurobanking/Eurodollar world; second, and at the same time, the problem of international debt as it concerns the Tier III countries must be defused. Because the two problem areas overlap, these changes are both more necessary and more possible. As Howard Wachtel pointed out,

> Quieting worldwide financial instability requires a strategy that simultaneously addresses both the Eurodollar overhang and Third World debt, in the context of a re-regulation of international money. . . . The debt owed at the end of 1984 by less-developed countries, Eastern European nations, and the Soviet Union to private supranational banks cannot be repaid in its present form. The time horizon is too short for the debtor nations to accumulate the hard currency they need to pay off this amount of debt in the austere, monetarist economic environment that pervades the world economy. The consequence is a lunging from crisis to crisis that is destabilizing for both debtor and creditor nations. To extricate ourselves from this game of chicken being played with blindfolds requires an institutionalized process of orderly debt rescheduling.[5]

The Eurodollar overhang was in embryo form already in the late 1950s. The United States, running balance-of-payments deficits as the result of rising investment and military spending abroad (constituting a demand for foreign currencies), forcefully persuaded its economic and political "partners" to accumulate dollars as, in effect, IOUs without a repayment date. Thus the United States was allowed to pay for its overseas expenditures with paper rather than goods and services. In turn, the Europeans sought ways to gain income on their ever-accumulating dollars. By the late 1960s, U.S. foreign spending having risen with increasing rapidity (not least for the war in Vietnam, but also for rising direct investments in Europe), the embryo had become a lusty adult; today it is a giant run amok. What underlay this extraordinary development was the combination of U.S. foreign spending, European desire to gain rather than to lose from it, and (given this background) most important, the fact that the U.S. banking system works within reserve (among other) requirements and the fact that the emerging Eurobank/Eurodollar system was and is entirely free from *any* requirements.

The critical development came when major U.S. banks, seeking to enhance their profits and evade U.S. controls, found the way to join in the European scramble. It was the negotiable certificate of deposit, which now can be seen as a ticket of admission to financial chaos. R. T. Naylor explained it as follows:

> The critical innovation of the major American banks to gain access to the growing pool of hot and homeless money was a piece of paper called a negotiable certificate of deposit (CD). Introduced by Citibank in 1961, a CD in effect (though not in law) was a security the bank could sell to a corporation or individual with a temporary surplus of cash. The buyer could either hold it to maturity and pick up all accrued interest, or, if short of money in the interim, sell it back to the bank at a slight penalty or to a third party. The CD [thus] gave banks an entry into the long-term capital market . . . [where] they could compete with governments and corporations trying to raise money through the sale of bills and bonds. Then, in 1964, the CD became cosmopolitan . . . when Citibank issue[d] a "eurodollar" CD. Thus emerged the financial instrument that would be critical to the banks' penetration of the offshore pool of dollar liquidity that subsequently became known as the eurodollar market [which has no reserve requirements]. Because of the lack of reserve requirements, banks can lend deposits back and forth to each other, puffing the hypothetical value of assets/liabilities on their books almost with impunity . . . ; [this] allows *all* the deposits to be rechanneled into interest-bearing loans. That in turn permits the eurobanks to offer depositors higher rates of interest than would be possible on domestically booked business. Lack of regulation also means complete anonymity . . . to depositors.[6]

It is more than ironic that the Eurodollars are a child of the cold war. When the Chinese Communists won their revolution, in 1949, they anticipated (correctly) that the United States would freeze China's dollar deposits. To avoid that, the Chinese quickly deposited their dollars in a Soviet bank in Paris. Subsequently, the Soviets began to deposit their own dollars in a Soviet bank in London. From this bizarre beginning, involving trivial amounts of dollars (when measured against the global financial system), the "Euromarket" has taken one step or another to find its present function as a whirlpool of speculation, involving over $1 trillion of assets/liabilities—a multiple of the dollars circulating in the United States itself. It is estimated that global financial transactions average at least $150 billion *per day*, well under 10 percent of that sum relating to trade in goods and services.

The principal reason for both the popularity and the dangers of this system is, of course, that it is a high-rolling international crap game. The main losers from this game, however, have not been and are unlikely to be the daily players. The system is a key target for reform. An international authority for such purposes has an attractive ring to it, as does "world government," even when the authority proposed is the IMF (which has done so much damage already), strengthened and changed in order to administer a reserve requirement system. But the British economist Susan Strange was probably correct when she argued:

> The United States is the only country that is in a position to regulate the operations of international banks, whether they are British, German, or Japanese. This is primarily because of the unquenchable preference of buyers and sellers, creditors and debtors, traders and bankers for dealing in U.S. dollars rather than any other currency . . . [which] has survived both extremes of the volatile foreign exchange markets, both the years when the dollar was objectively . . . far too weak and . . . when it has been far too strong.[7]

Because the largest and most active financial markets are in the United States and major financial innovations occur there, the enormous and increasing flows of international finance going through the New York Clearing House (NYCH) system, according to Strange, "give the United States a unique opportunity to develop the role of international lender of last resort."[8] Her proposal is thus, *not* for an international authority to act as a central bank, which is politically implausible, but for the United States to use its still great power to employ its existing institutions (the Federal Reserve System, in addition to the NYCH) as that de facto authority. The rest of the world would acquiesce for simple reasons of profit and convenience, without ever having to come to its senses.

Such a development would require that key political and financial powers in the United States begin to come to their senses, however.

Considering that Wall Street is the Las Vegas of the global financial system, and that many of the relevant key political and financial powers, far from being likely to place themselves in the lead of a reform process, are instead those whose actions have contributed to an intensification of the problem, this or any other kind of financial reform has a ring of fantasy to it. However, there are some glimmers of hope: Personalities such as Felix Rohatyn who are important in the financial sector are appropriately alarmed and open to reform. Citibank, in taking steps to (in effect) write off a good share of its Tier III loans in 1987, showed that it was paying some attention to the realities of current financial processes.[9] If such glimmers of hope are to become more substantial, all concerned must be aware of a set of connected changes in which they could see their own altered policies as being in their interest. That includes not only Tier III debt reform, to be taken up next, but also the whole group of proposals concerned with production, with goods and services, to be examined later. As this debt reform is discussed, it will be assumed that some effective stabilization of finance along the lines above will be simultaneously under way.

Tier III Debt Reform

A calming of global financial waters would in itself be at least modestly helpful for reducing Tier III debt problems to manageable proportions, as, vice versa, the kinds of proposals concerning those debts, were they to be implemented, would help to calm the global waters. However, no matter how far such financial reforms are taken, they would leave unaddressed the urgent problem of how to increase the earning capacities of Tier III nations so that, within the reformed financial system, they could both pay off (or be freed from) debt *and* improve their production and incomes. Just as some stabilization of finance in connection with Tier III debt reforms was assumed so should some basic changes in the "real" processes of consumption, production, trade, and investment (to be proposed later) be assumed.

Tier III debt, it must be recognized at the outset, cannot be viewed through the same analytical (or judgmental) lenses as ordinary household, business, or government debt. It originated in partially unique ways, it was used (and misused) in ways unique to its sector, and the obligations associated with the debt (especially interest payments) have taken on their dimensions for reasons beyond Tier III's control or responsibility. Any approach to Tier III debt that neglects these matters is bound to fail. To understand the way that Tier III debt problems are different from other types of debt problems, the following position should be kept in mind: "The most important question should not be *how* a developing [i.e., Tier III] country might pay the debt service charges being demanded but *why* it should—or perhaps should not."[10]

A predictable response to that query, especially from those free-market apostles who dominate economic thought and behavior today, would emphasize the choices made by debtors and the services provided by creditors and see any suggestion of partial, let alone nonpayment, as some combination of criminality on the part of the debtors and misguided charity or idealism on the part of the creditors. But Tier III debt and what underlies and surrounds it were not a creation of the free market or anything that can be dignified with the word *choice*. Where should I begin to support this argument?

First, it may be said that it is the people of the Tier III nations who have been paying and must continue to pay the interest (and if paid, the principal). But the countries of Tier III are at their best only remotely characterized by representative government and are at their worst, which is close to typical, one form or another of dictatorship, militarized and corrupt from top to bottom. As the IMF and other agencies impose "austerity" programs on such countries to assure (in vain) debt repayment (which has come to mean interest only), it is neither the people who negotiated the loans nor those who benefited from them (as businessmen, as corrupt government officials, as swindlers, or as capital flight/Swiss bank account specialists) who pay. It is the population that pays—with lowered social benefits and wages and rising unemployment.[11]

Second, most loans to Tier III countries (like global oil prices) are denominated in dollars and, frequently, contracted for in terms that assure "variable" (upward) interest rates. After the early 1970s, oil prices, interest rates, and the dollar broke through the ceiling; the downward movement of all these by the late 1980s was accompanied by falling prices for Tier III exports and falling volumes of export. Heads they lose, tails they lose.

Third, although a good portion of Tier III borrowing, despite all, was done in the name of developmental projects in the 1960s and 1970s (the decades of most of the initial borrowing), in the 1980s almost all the new loans were negotiated simply to keep from sinking, or for balance-of-payments financing, for maintaining interest payments, and the like. Much of the reason why this was necessary had to do with a severe deterioration in the terms of trade for Tier III countries (exporters of raw materials, mostly, who had to export more to pay interest and/ or to import the same amount as before) associated with the engineered recession of 1981–1982 and associated rising interest rates and the strong dollar.[12]

Fourth, and a matter to be turned to in later pages, the Tier III countries have been made a part of a general world power struggle that has led them, like the United States and other major powers, to waste a good percentage of their economic strength on military material and activities. The world struggle is mirrored in Tier III indirectly (as in Angola), whatever the wishes of all parties concerned, but that is often only a pretext, as when a Tier III society seeking to break loose from a colonial and oppressed past (as in Guatemala) is encouraged and assisted in becoming (or remaining) a military dictatorship to prevent its change. Not only are military expenditures disproportionately high, but they are in fact used to prevent badly needed social and economic and political change. The responsibility for that lies at the door of those who pay the piper, not always, but most often, the United States.[13]

Whether with respect to debt or to incomes and production, the needs of the Tier III countries are critical not just for the well-being of their own people but also for the entire world. Depressed economic levels in those countries reduce the markets for badly needed exports from Tiers I and II and become part of a vicious cycle of decline, a cycle that now has an explosive financial component in it. And if and when a major war breaks out, it is likely that it will have its beginnings in Tier III, which includes, after all, the Middle East, Central America, and Africa. Consequently, although the immediate needs for financial reform are vital and must be met, so too are the needs for a long-term alteration of the political economy of Tier III countries, within them and between them and the world economy.

There have been proposals for reform since 1982, when the Tier III debt crisis became public. Although there is some overlap between the proposals originating in Tiers I and II, and those from Tier III, there is much more in the way of sharp contrast, in both what is talked about and how it is seen. The "reformers" from Tiers I and II tend to talk only about very recent and very near-future financial questions, whereas those from Tier III have a temporal framework that stretches far back and far forward, and they argue that the real worlds of production, consumption, trade, and investment must also be part of any workable "package" of changes. The creditors view their debtors as a teacher might see a naughty child or a lazy one; the debtors probe what they see as the fundamental defects of the school system.

Thus, from the powerful nations, there are proposals to lend more, within an accepted framework of austerity (the poor become poorer, that the rich may collect their debts). There are more liberal proposals to put ceilings on interest payments ("interest capping"), for collective loan insurance (for the creditors), for a public loan authority to raise capital to refinance and support a significant share of shaky debts. So go the proposals from Tiers I and II. Even if these proposals were all to be implemented fully, they would serve as palliatives that might reduce the fever but leave the illness unabated. Meanwhile, the lenders and the IMF and governments (especially the U.S. Treasury) "restructure," which means doling out billions here and there to allow interest payments to continue and Tiers I and II to postpone bank failures, and the IMF (and behind it, the lenders and others) requires an impossible and cruel austerity program.

Debt and its problems are larger and more critical in Latin America than elsewhere in Tier III, and attention has rightly been focused more there. Meetings bringing together various Latin American nations have been held, and others called for, but the actions that have been taken have been individual—to the vast relief of the creditor nations, whose greatest fear is a "debtors' cartel." On the financial side alone, Mexico was the first to be involved in restructuring, in 1982 (as discussed earlier), and then there were others: Argentina, Brazil, Bolivia, Ecuador, Colombia. Peru took an early independent stand when it proclaimed (in 1985) that it would limit its debt repayments to an amount not exceeding 10 percent of its foreign exchange earnings (about one-fourth of the average in that part of the world). In February 1987, Brazil stopped interest payments on about 60 percent of its debt and has subsequently (until 1988, without success) sought to restructure in its own way, by having its debt written down, refinanced, and its repayment in effect postponed (through long-term bonds). Next to the United States, Brazil (owing over $112 billion) is the largest debtor in the world. Then comes Mexico, then Argentina. The latter has been able to postpone the payment date on over half of its debt, with rescheduled loans and moratoria. Mexico's meetings to restructure and borrow more are becoming annual affairs. And so it goes: The problem, clearly not dealt with and always increasing. The debtors are able to "twist the arms" of the creditors, up to a point; the creditors are learning to write down loans. Meanwhile, the economies of Tier III sink from their low levels to depths not experienced since the 1930s. It is like the problem of many farmers in the United States.

And like those farmers in the United States, the economies of Tier III need considerably more than a conventional financial approach to their problems. The approach that is needed goes well beyond anything coming from Tiers I and II as actions or proposals, varying from "reclassification" of debts in terms of who incurred how much for what (for example, should the people of the Philippine Islands be held responsible for the debts incurred by Ferdinand Marcos and his gang, or should the bankers, or the U.S. government?), or when the debt was incurred and what part of the resulting interest burden is due to engineered recession, terms-of-trade deterioration (the Reagan administration takes credit for the recession of 1981–1982 and its lowering of inflation), and associated great increases in interest rates. In other words, the question raised earlier must be dealt with: not only how and when a developing country should pay off its debts, but *whether* it should. The answer to that question will not come from academic debates but from the ability of the Tier III countries to learn to represent themselves together, or from their inability to do so.

They have done so already in modest ways, almost always through one agency or another of the United Nations—a major reason why the United States (among others) continually downplays or ignores those agencies. Going back to the 1950s, the proposal for a Commodity Stabilization Fund (which would stabilize Tier III export prices in something like the manner used for Tier I and II agricultural prices) was put forth. In moderating frequent and sharp fluctuations of commodity prices (coffee, tin, et cetera), both the buyers and sellers could be better off, as could also be true if prices were stabilized at a fair level. Nothing has come of that proposal, except, one might say, the efforts of individual commodity groups such as OPEC. Another proposal on the "real" level has been that for a Special United Nations Fund for Economic Development (SUNFED); it died stillborn in the 1960s as, in the 1980s, did the World Development Fund (of the Brandt Commission). The most recent proposal (the meetings concerning it were officially boycotted by the United States—alone in the United Nations) was to apply some percentage of the savings from whatever disarmament might be in the offing to a development fund for Tier III countries. (Although very few citizens of the United States would know it, the first time such a proposal was aired was in the 1950s, by then-President Eisenhower.)

None of these proposals from the weaker countries has gotten anywhere, nor are any likely to. What has been proposed is all necessary, and so is a good deal more. The problem is not one that has to do with good sense or necessity; it has to do with power and politics, to getting those with much and those with very little power to understand, to accept, and to work for needed and workable—and generally beneficial—changes. A changed outlook is required to bring about changed institutions; unlike disaster, change will not just happen, it must be wrought. And none of this is possible unless it fits within the main needs and rhythms of the present system, meeting the needs in altered ways. That question must be confronted now directly. Then it will be possible to proceed to more basic changes.

Back to Fundamentals

To have any claim whatsoever to realism, all proposals for change (1) must take due account of the main capitalist imperatives, modifying while maintaining exploitation, expansion, and concentrated power; and (2) because of the critical role of military spending both as problem and opportunity, any proposals for its reduction and conversion to civilian uses must confront at least some of the dimensions of the cold war, including its involvement with the Tier III nations.

Military expenditures in the United States since World War II have always been enormous; since 1978, beginning before Reagan and accelerated by him even more, they have risen in both absolute and relative terms. Now approximating $300 billion a year (the request is always for more than that), they are the highest in the world, as usual. But the United States accounts for "only" about a third of global military spending. The poorest countries of the world (excluding China) account for about a fifth of total spending, in addition to suffering the destruction that comes from its use.[14]

The foregoing constitutes the basis for my principal proposal: an initially significant and then a continuing reduction of military expenditures throughout the world. The principle, not the exact amount, is the point at issue. For purposes of this discussion, let us assume an initial one-third decrease in current worldwide military spending. That would allow the world to go on spending between $600 and $700 billion in the first year for equipment and military personnel, and the military strength of all would continue to increase. Both for economic and political reasons, joined to that change is the vital proviso that *non*military governmental spending would rise to the same amount. Were that not so, the proposal would be utterly unrealistic, especially for the United States, whose economy would swiftly collapse, bringing the rest of the world down with it. (It is generally understood that the most recent U.S. "recovery," like so many before it, was fueled by the military-based budget deficits of the period.)

There are many problems associated with such a proposal, but they are not *economic* in nature, as that term is understood. They are problems, rather, that have to do with attitudes and politics, those that generated, arise from, and continue the cold war, on the one hand, and those that (usually implicitly) assume the current relationships between Tiers I and II and the nations of Tier III are appropriate, necessary, and desirable, on the other. And of course all the foregoing connect with each other as well.

The effectuation of the proposal to reduce military expenditures would assist in lessening tension between the major parties to the cold war—the United States, the USSR, and China—and putting that proposal into effect would require such lessening of tensions (the chicken and egg problem, it seems, but there are, after all, chickens and eggs, and there can be movement along the lines suggested). (Indeed, in 1988 there seemed to be better than a faint glimmering of hope.) But because so much of the world's military spending and activity are directly or indirectly part of Third World struggles, it is also necessary at the same time to initiate a transformation of the relationships between the major powers and Tier III. These relationships bear a critical dependence upon some combination of actual or threatened economic force and/or military violence, exploitation, and the creation and support of repressive governments. The largest part (though not all) of the Tier III repressive governments connects with Tiers I and II, the rest with the noncapitalist powers.

The substantial reduction of military expenditures, important in itself for both economic and political reasons, is also the key to possibilities of success in reducing waste (such as restricted production) and thereby increasing real incomes in the nonmilitary realm. Alongside that assertion stands another: Just as the reduction of military spending requires the reduction of political tension and allows the improvement of living standards (especially among the poorest), such reductions and improvements also make less worrisome the reduction of military spending— the opposite of a vicious circle.

Clearly no progress along these lines can be made without at least somewhat taming the cold war, while reducing the mutual fears of its main participants. But can the people and the present and potential leaders of the United States, the Soviet Union, and China come to see the futility, even the madness of the tendencies of the 1980s—more than rhetorically? There seems little doubt that the answer is positive, always excepting the hopelessly bellicose groups in these three (and other) countries. Such groups are both partial creators of and partially created by the cold war and its incessant propaganda, which, one may assume, would also be reduced significantly as changes were sought.

It is not a mark of political innocence to believe that the Soviet and Chinese people and leaders want a more peaceful world at least as much as those of the United States, although very few people in the United States seem at all aware of that. Of all the major powers, the United States was the least damaged by the two world wars and, a different matter, the most benefited. Total U.S. deaths from the two wars came to about 700,000. The Russians lost about 10 million people between 1914 and 1921, from war and civil war (the latter with military participation and financial support by the United States, Britain, and others, against the Soviet government). As a result of World War II, the Soviet Union lost at least 20 million people, out of a total of 60 million(!) deaths in all of Europe from the war years. After three-quarters of a century of terrible suffering from the waste, destruction, agonies, and displacement of war, who can doubt that the Soviet people ardently desire peace? To this it may be added that current Soviet leadership is quite conscious of two facts: (1) their economy must be improved so as to improve its productive capacities *and* raise real consumption levels; and (2) this cannot be done without lowering military expenditures.[15]

On the latter two points, there is little difference for China. Its historical process in this century has of course differed from that of the Soviet Union, but it has also been physically and socially devastating, for about the same number of decades. Bitter civil war stretched from at least the 1920s until its conclusion in 1949. Within that period invasion and war from Japan beginning in the early 1930s was sandwiched. And then China was involved in the Korean War. Furthermore, in addition to their long and expensive conflict with the United States since 1949, the substantial animosity and mutual fears between the Soviet Union and China (and their vast shared and disputed border areas) have meant a substantial military burden for China from the Soviet quarter alone. It is said that more troops and missiles face each other between China and the Soviet Union than toward the West, and it is known that China's extensive underground civil defense shelters have been extraordinarily costly in manpower and resources. It cannot be doubted that the Chinese are patently eager to modernize their very large economy, critically held back by the military drag.

That it is a drag has always been true for those two countries; it has never helped, instead it has always harmed their economies—as they, and the United States, have long known. In its distorting way, "military Keynesianism" *has* helped the U.S. economy, in the sense of preventing serious economic contraction and maintaining levels of profits and jobs otherwise out of reach. But one theme of this study is that the United States, indeed the entire capitalist world economy, now has reason to see that military spending and its side effects constitute an ever-enlarging source of problems, not solutions. In short, the United States and its so-called adversaries have an objective basis upon which to come to a meeting of minds, a basis that would have been quite implausible only a few years ago.

In their very different ways, Gorbachev and Reagan have made change possible: Gorbachev, because he has recognized and admitted Soviet weaknesses and knows that *glasnost* and *perestroika* cannot go beyond slim hopes without significant demilitarization of the Soviet economy; Reagan, because in extending the military rhetoric and spending to the breaking point, he has revealed the limits of both. And just as Reagan was said to have wanted to "go out with a good last act," Gorbachev won't last long without a strong "first act." Quite apart from these representative developments, it has become clear to a broadening circle of people of all functions and at all levels that the extraordinarily expensive military hardware of the late 1980s cannot be afforded by *any* society. For the same reasons that the time for change appears increasingly necessary, it appears increasingly possible.

The United States is the pivotal nation in the capitalist world, critically positioned if there is to be any movement toward reducing cold war tensions and military spending. It has now become a commonplace in financial and economic analysis that present levels of both private consumption and military spending in the United States are financed by borrowing from the rest of the world (especially from Japan, which purchases about one-third or more of U.S. Treasury offerings, month after month) and that in a basic sense the nation can no longer develop either a monetary or fiscal policy that ignores its need to attract foreign investment, real or financial. In an economy constantly flirting with recession, it is particularly dangerous for the Fed to have to "tune" interest rates upward with that in mind. And with or without Reagan, some time soon taxes must go up and real consumption must decline. There is an alternative, namely, maintaining taxes while lowering military expenditures and raising others, which can pay for needed goods and services (and reduce waste).

Turning to such possibilities, one must remind oneself that any and all attempts to halt or reverse the arms race will encounter accumulated distrust and fears, both absurd and plausible, in all the affected countries. For present purposes, it is both necessary and appropriate to approach this question as it exists in the United States.

Something Old, Something New

The general public, business, unions, and politicians all must become open to the belief that there are constructive and safe economic *and* political alternatives to the cold war and to military expenditures and interventionism over the globe. Jerry Sanders put it concisely and well when he wrote that the changes made by and in the United States must *at least* "include a broad populist appeal that provides for the economic and political participation of the previously disenfranchised, a lasting social contract that guarantees protection and stability to those in the precarious middle of the social spectrum, and a firm commitment to the industrial innovation and technological modernization that will open up the economic and educational opportunities of the future."[16]

The practical-minded and well-intentioned, especially if they are economists, object to thinking along lines that imply the possibilities of general improvement, even in the United States, let alone much of the rest of the world. Perhaps the most listened-to voice in this respect is that of Lester Thurow—perhaps one of the top two or three U.S.

economists in ability, and almost always focused on vital problems such as economic change, income distribution, and deindustrialization. It is he who emphasized that the economic process is a zero-sum game. And he insisted that "there *are* solutions for each of our problem areas. We do not face a world of unsolvable problems. But while there are solutions in each case, these solutions have a common characteristic. Each requires that some large group—sometimes a minority and sometimes the majority—be willing to tolerate a large reduction in their real standard of living."[17]

Quite so, if the economy is operating at reasonably full employment of labor and of agricultural and industrial productive capacity, and if the composition of production is devoid of significant waste (in the form of what is produced, and how, and whether). Like so many economists (and others) who seek or who resist change in the capitalist system, Thurow focused on income distribution—and he rightly rejected that as a feasible tool of lasting change. Of all capitalist institutions, the distribution of income (and of wealth) is the most intransigent to all but very short-term change, except, perhaps, upward. But the focus in this book is upon *waste* and the conversion of wasted production and resources into things useful and needed. If waste is reduced, distribution may remain the same and everyone be better off. In the jargon of economics, such a process would be Pareto efficient, that is, nobody need be worse off (except perhaps in injured feelings), and everybody could be better off. There is that much waste.[18]

Continuing with sets of linked and mutually supporting proposals for change, it is important to note that ends and means are often indistinguishable from each other. For example, to convince people in the United States that a reduction of military spending will not harm their job and income possibilities, it would be necessary to have an offsetting program of, let us say, housing construction. The latter is a desirable end in itself, given the substantial housing shortage for middle- and low-income families. It is also a means for increasing jobs and aiding business, as well as a means for making reductions in military spending acceptable on economic grounds, in turn facilitating a reduction in global tensions—good in itself.

The general domestic policies to accompany a program of reduced military spending (the focus here is on the United States) have been put forth by many academic and political individuals and groups in recent years. In some cases they are a revival, deepening, and broadening of New Deal policies; in others, especially when the call is for re-industrialization, a response to the weakened state of the U.S. economy in the world and at home. Here is a selection from the proposals of Alan Wolfe. Among other changes, he argued the need for:

- a commitment to full employment and the creation of a government agency that would guarantee it by subsidizing the movement of workers into jobs in productive, community-sunrise [that is, growing] industries.
- price controls . . . to control inflation in the necessities. . . . Prices are too important to be left to those who raise them.
- reindustrialization. The federal government must be given the authority to encourage balanced growth in highly productive new industries that serve social needs. A . . . program based on shop-floor participation . . . is more compatible with increasing productivity than one based on self-serving deals between conservative union bureaucrats and even more conservative managers.
- job training. The first priority of social policy should be to train those who need skills for the jobs they will have if an industrial policy is created premised upon full employment.
- alternative delivery modes. Under the imperatives of growth politics, the middle class paid taxes to support the delivery of services more than the services themselves. Huge bureaucracies, cost-plus contracts, and unsound financial practices lay behind housing and health policies. Domestic policy can be made to respond to social needs if it encourages delivery systems that have political and fiscal integrity. Rehabilitating existing housing stock; providing community-based day-care centers and self-help medical care; eliminating the welfare bureaucracy; and banning the construction of new urban highways—these kinds of programs would prevent the hostility and resentment that were the inevitable result of using the rhetoric of helping the poor to line the pockets of the rich.[19]

Combining all these policies with the establishment of a floor beneath which real incomes (decent shelter, food, health care, education) would not be allowed to sink would constitute long strides toward greater economic stability and well-being for the entire nation. Far from being utopian, such policies are already the norm in capitalist Scandinavia and substantially in place in other nations of Western Europe, not least in West Germany.[20]

Connected with programs for reducing military spending and reforming the domestic social economy could and should be the altered use of existing productive capacities in industry and agriculture. Long-standing dependence upon artificially created shortages is demonstrably self-defeating, whether the agency of restricted production is the government or giant corporations acting collusively. The failures of output restriction are best known as they refer to agriculture, for there it is the popular image of the family farm in trouble, despite its hard work, and so forth, that makes the evening TV screen. The situation in industry has been equally desperate, when measured in jobs lost and workers downgraded; it is just as much a tragedy, but not so appealing (or so easy to portray) on the TV screen. In any case, the apparent successes of the two decades or so after 1950 have now come to their end; and restricted production only benefits those who survive. As time passes, the survivors are well outnumbered by those who have been cast aside.

Clearly, those who have been cast aside will not be brought back to the cornucopia of plenty by a continuing status quo. Means must be developed both to enlarge domestic and foreign markets for the products of agriculture and industry and to alter the structure of the service industry. The waste that is represented by underutilized productive capacities and labor can be reduced through governmental programs that steadily replace spending on military production with programs that allow increased expenditures on nonmilitary production. The argument's main thread, therefore, is that through the careful and steady conversion of useless to useful production, the wasteful practices in agriculture, industry, and the services can be turned to more sensible and badly needed processes. What can and will happen with military production is to be decided in the political realm, and that amounts to saying that what can happen with underutilization will be the consequence of integrally related political efforts and decisions, decisions that seek to change the levels of consumption at home and abroad, and most especially in Tier III countries.

It must be seen as axiomatic that to reduce military spending substantially depends upon a simultaneous program to convert its effective productive capacities to private consumption and investment. Every ingredient of a program to guide the present crisis toward a beneficial direction requires political effort and change; in turn, it also requires the kind of energy and political education that made the cold war and contemporary capitalism possible. Neither of those two sprang up overnight, nor will changes for the better. Farmers and businesses and workers in industry and politicians have been fooled, one may say, and have also fooled themselves. However, who is to say that, faced with beneficial alternatives to the present course toward disaster, all those people would prefer increasingly costly foolishness to a convincingly hopeful set of alternatives?

Arithmetic and Life and Death

Assume a military budget for the United States of $300 billion; then assume a reduction of that by one-third, roughly the U.S. share of what was earlier posited for global military reductions. Assume further a total federal budget of about $1 trillion (the present level). Federal social spending capacities (assuming no change in the level of total government spending) would increase by more than the apparent 10 percent ($100 billion as a share of $1 trillion); military capacity would not be reduced, but its rate of increase would merely be slowed. This is so because only about one-third of the total budget covers "social expenditures": social insurance, aid to farmers and small business, transportation, health, education; the rest goes to military and paramilitary (national security) programs, and "government operations" (about $140 billion of which is for interest on the federal debt). In other words, the savings from a reduction of military spending of one-tenth of the total budget could increase social spending by about one-third—or more, if agricultural support programs were made less necessary by other output- and demand-increasing changes. Also one should note that employment and income-enhancing programs would broaden and deepen the tax base: Many more jobs would be gained than lost if nonmilitary production took the place of military spending, as numerous academic, congressional, and union studies have demonstrated. That the quality of life would improve can also be taken for granted.

Over the span of ten years or so, if the nations of the world were to engage in a gradual and steady program of demilitarization of production, the compounded "military dividend," as President Eisenhower once called it, could easily amount to over $1 trillion worth of released production and effective purchasing power (directly and/or through subsidization). Conversion of militarily wasted labor and productive capacities and resources would by themselves account for a large part of that trillion. If one also were to anticipate further changes in the nonmilitarized sectors of the world economy, changes that would eliminate waste, economic possibilities for a sensible and decent world could improve substantially more.

Take agriculture: The Food and Agriculture Organization of the United Nations has long estimated that at least 500 million people are desperately hungry, malnourished, and close to starvation over the globe. The 1986 United Nations Children's Fund (UNICEF) report on "The State of the World's Children" underscored this ongoing tragedy particularly vividly when it declared: "Almost without notice, more than 14 million children are now dying every year . . . , in the final coma of dehydration . . . ; in the extremities of respiratory infections . . . ; in the grip of tetanus spasms . . . ; of frequent and ordinary illnesses which steadily weaken and malnourish the body until it has nothing left to fight the next cold, the next fever or the next bout of diarrhoea."[21] That means 280,000 children a week, or 40,000 each day of the year, 2 children per second of every hour. UNICEF estimated in 1981 that $100 spent on the 500 million poorest children and their mothers would provide basic health assistance, elementary education, care during pregnancy, diet improvement, and a hygienic water supply. That is, $50 billion, or 5 percent of present global military expenditures could not only save, it could effectively enrich, who knows how many lives. The costs of the MX missile and B-1 bomber fiascoes (both of them more costly each year and more dysfunctional, the public learns), among other such boondoggles, must be measured in the lives that could be saved with their billions.[22] But one must also look inside the universal practices of agriculture for what amounts to social insanity.

There are at least two major scandals in world agriculture. One keeps prices up, causing consumers to pay more in the market and then to pay also as taxpayer for the privilege of paying higher prices, while countless numbers, unable to pay market prices (but perhaps paying some part of the taxes), go hungry. The other is that the supply of foodstuffs could be so very much greater. Farmers would like it to increase, if not to their detriment, of course. And it could increase, not with a "free market," which modern farming cannot allow, but with policies designed to produce abundance and low prices instead of market scarcity and high prices.

The suggestions made here have been proposed in the past or function in the present (in countries such as Sweden). Thus, in the United States in 1948, a time of uncertainty as to the future and of fearful memories of the very recent and terribly depressed past, then–Secretary of Agriculture William Brannan proposed a plan that would have maintained the incomes of those with small and middle-sized farms, would have increased production, and would have lowered food prices. His plan would have established a floor for farm incomes, both absolutely and proportionate to production, and also a ceiling for financial returns from the program. It would have let production run free and let the market decide, which would have meant falling prices. The program—the Brannan Plan—was derided as "milk for the Hottentots," by those at the top of the agricultural pyramid (by "farmers" like Senator James Eastland of Mississippi, with his 100,000 acres and million-dollar government checks—obtained in exchange for his limiting his own cotton production), and by not a few nonrich farmers who opposed government handouts. Such handouts (though perhaps better disguised) are what farmers receive through price support programs.

Because, after so many decades of the latter programs, farmers now view themselves as an endangered species, the time may be ripe to renew such proposals. The Brannan Plan, squashed as though it were a stinging wasp, was as striking in its good sense and its social decency as current programs (in and outside the United States) are in their poor sense and social injustice. Such a worthwhile program was practiced in Britain until its membership in the European Common Market forced that country to adopt its current price support programs. Despite all the programs that have been practiced in the name of preserving the small farmer, the numbers of small farmers steadily decline. The program of Brannan could be revived, both in the United States and elsewhere. Everyone would be better off, including, probably, those already rich. It should not be beyond the wit of the human species to find a way to use all its food-producing capacities in a world that desperately needs food, and to do so in a way that benefits farmers and consumers both. As the saying goes, If we can put a man on the moon. . . .

As it could be for farmers, so it could be for industrial production, although the latter presents a more complicated set of problems. Even with the enormous amounts of military production of the past decades, the tendency toward global overcapacity and serious unemployment has continued to increase. And unemployment tends to rise in the leading countries because of the ways in which industrialists seek to solve the problem: by "outsourcing" (having parts, et cetera, produced in, generally, Tier III factories), and by partially or wholly closing plants in Tiers I and II. As mentioned earlier, manufacturing firms (in autos, electronics, textiles, steel) prefer to use their equipment at around 85 percent of capacity, seen as an "optimum" rate for overall efficiency. Some representative conditions were cited by the *Wall Street Journal* (March 9, 1987), under the heading: "Glutted Markets: A Global Overcapacity Hurts Many Industries; No Easy Cure is Seen." *Item:* Automotive demand is in the low 30s (of millions/annum), while productive capacity is in the low to mid-40s and rising. *Item:* Steel's annual global overcapacity runs between 75 and 200 million metric tons, with total capacity of 570 million metric tons. It was estimated that "*only* if the entire U.S. steel industry shut down would demand equal supply in the non-Communist world." *Item:* Semiconductors' equipment use rate went from 100 percent in 1984 to about 60 percent in 1985 and is at about 70 percent in 1987. *Item:* "Makers of farm and construction equipment are buried in overcapacity but, surprisingly, some countries, especially South Korea, are nonetheless believed to be planning more plants." (South Korea is also adding to automotive capacity and in keeping with other countries and other industries, is acting normally within the nationally and globally unplanned system of investment and production.) The *Journal's* list went on, with oil, and textiles, and nonferrous metals, and computers, and more.

As stagnation afflicts the markets for commodities, it has its consequences in rising unemployment, whose long-term trend has been upward. In the United States, unemployment hovered around 3.5 percent in the late 1960s; in the early 1970s, it was between 4 and 6 percent; by the late 1970s, it was between 6 and 9 percent; and in the early 1980s, it was between 7 and 10+ percent. With the longest sustained postwar recovery since 1983, the level has finally been pushed down to below

6 percent. These are the data of stagnation, both despite and because of enormous military spending and enormous deficits. What has been true in the United States has been true elsewhere, although with different numbers (some higher, some lower, all seen as serious in their countries—in Japan, for example, whose 3 percent unemployment rate occasions fears that might result from a 12 percent rate in the United States).

It should be clear from the foregoing that military spending has not prevented the development of excess capacity or unemployment, although it is equally clear that, without that spending or compensating nonmilitary governmental spending, the process would have become considerably worse for both industry and workers. The only long-term *and* short-term solution is to find ways to use existing productive capacity and labor constructively. This means conversion. Conversion is not new; it has gone both ways in recent decades, for example, converting typewriter to machine gun production for World War II, as well as auto factories to airplane and tank production. And after the war, back again. Here, as in virtually everything discussed in this connection, the problem is not economic, or practical, but political. It is a matter of political power and will.

The initiatives for change must begin and continue in the political arena. Businesses (and workers) know all too well that what they produce cannot easily find adequate markets. It is also well known that the goods and services needed by society but unavailable in appropriate quantity or quality will not appear without politically facilitated changes. If there is to be an alteration from private to more public transportation, it must be instigated by government; likewise, for having fewer service stations and more housing, fewer guns and more food. It is especially obvious that the government is the central agency for change with respect to waste in the service sector. In that area, there are always more and more people pushing paper and hamburgers and brooms, and always too few providing for human needs.

The long-term trend of unemployment has been rising for twenty years, but so has employment, of course. What is striking is that unemployment has emerged in largest part from layoffs in the high-skill, high-pay, relatively secure unionized jobs; employment has grown principally in the other end of the job picture: low-skill, low-pay, relatively insecure, and nonunionized. *Item:* "The *increase* in employment in eating and drinking places since 1973 is greater than total employment in the automobile and steel industries combined."[23] That was written in 1981. Since then, employment in steel and autos has gone down by almost half, while the increase in service jobs has accelerated. Had it not, unemployment would of course be substantially higher. Sixty percent of all new jobs since 1981 have been at incomes less than $7,000/year in the United States: dead-end and deadly jobs.

There has never been a time in the United States when health and educational services (or other social services) have been adequate to meet people's needs, although in the 1960s some changes in a hopeful direction began to take hold (within an inadequate framework and outlook however).[24] In the same years in which the economy has moved into stagnation and crisis, those always-inadequate levels have been pushed down, steadily erasing what progress had been made. In the area of health care, the 1980s have seen an increase in uninsured costs along with an increase in fees and premiums, especially harsh on the old and the poor. In education during the same period, depressing tendencies were at work on all levels: overcrowded classrooms, inadequate facilities, shortened terms, badly paid staff, a great increase in part-time and nonbenefit jobs, and a spreading demoralization—for teachers, students, and staff. Students, both for these and other reasons stemming from the larger process of social neglect and recklessness, aptly reflect the defects of their schools and society and are held responsible for their own victimization.[25]

Is it not obvious that the U.S. public does *not* need the number of fast-food joints it has, let alone more and more and more of the same, and is it not equally obvious that it does need more and better and less expensive health care, child-care centers, civilized facilities for old people, and an educational system that helps the young to understand themselves, their society, and nature, and to appreciate and cherish them all? There are of course literally millions of young people (and not so young people) eager to be trained to fill the jobs that would provide the services needed—teachers, librarians, nurses, doctors, engineers, scientists. Instead, to become one of the "best brains" of the society is to develop and use skills for selling and speculating, even for killing; to become a yuppie, an individualist running rampant. In 1939, Budd Schulberg wrote the impressive and widely read novel *What Makes Sammy Run?* about a copyboy who lied and cheated and bullied his way to becoming a Hollywood producer, ruining everyone who stood in his way. In a recent interview, Schulberg stated that nowadays young people see Sammy as a model, as a hero. After a recent college talk, he recounted that a student came to him and said, of Sammy, "I love him. I felt a little nervous about going out into the world and making it. But reading *Sammy* gives me confidence. It's my bible." Life imitating art.[26] But it is reasonable to believe that a change of direction in society would bring out those capacities for useful work that are contained in all people.

R. H. Tawney spent much of his life studying capitalism, its origins, its history, its ways and means, its social philosophy. After World War

I, as Britain entered its long period of stagnation, as Germany combined stupefying inflation (a rise in prices of four *trillion* times between 1918 and 1923) with social decadence, as Italy began its tortured experience with fascism, and as the United States was euphorically embarked on its Jazz Age, Tawney, despairing of a society in which social optimism consisted of believing that "Greed is held in check by greed, and the desire for gain sets limits for itself," wrote: "It is obvious indeed, that no change of system or machinery can avert those causes of social *malaise* which consist in the egotism, greed, or quarrelsomeness of human nature. But what it can do is to create an environment in which those are not the qualities which are encouraged. It cannot secure that men live up to their principles. What it can do is establish their social order upon principles to which, if they please, they can live up and not live down."[27]

Neither force nor greed has ever been absent from history, of course, but in the capitalist process of recent years such ends and means have changed from being present to becoming the virtual dynamic of the system. The consequence is not only that the world economy is in crisis but also that society is hell-bent on economic disaster and a spread and evolution of current conflicts into a nuclear disaster as well. Both the economic and the military situations are likely to explode first in the Tier III countries, plagued by debt, exploitation, external manipulation, poverty, oppression, violence, and (usually) corrupt and dictatorial rule. If all the proposals made up to this point were implemented, their promise would be dangerously limited unless they were accompanied by substantial and concurrent changes in the economic, military, and political relationships between Tier III and the powerful nations. I shall close with that focus and argue that along with and because of decreased militarization, there can and there must be decreased exploitation and control of the Tier III countries and their people.

Justice as Necessity

Since the late 1940s, the United States has seen itself as the architect and saviour of the "free world" as well as promoter of the economic development of Tier III countries. Symmetrically, the Soviet Union and China (among others, such as Cuba) have been portrayed as malevolent forces seeking to undermine or sidetrack both freedom and development. Supporting these beliefs have been some astonishing numbers and policies: Between 1946 and 1988, in addition to its several trillion dollars of military expenditures, the United States has had over 300 major military bases abroad (over 2,000, counting major and minor), a network of close to 400 treaties covering the globe, and has threatened or carried out military intervention in over 200 instances, not counting covert or paramilitary operations such as the creation and support of the Contras in Nicaragua, the overthrow of elected governments (Iran, 1953; Guatemala, 1954), and the like. Neither the Soviet Union nor China could have afforded such far-reaching and costly actions, whether or not it had the inclination.[28]

As a consequence of U.S. policies in Tier III, not only did the United States very much affect the nature and functioning of the governments of a very large percentage of those countries, it also provided itself with privileged access to resources, markets, and investment outlets, often at the expense of former European (or Japanese) masters, as well as the people of Tier III. Like the population of the imperial powers of the past, a good share of the U.S. population doubtless thinks (or senses) that its well-being depends upon the cheap labor and raw materials that characterize Tier III. But now many Americans are coming to believe that their unemployment and insecurity have the same origin. The time for changed political minds may be approaching. But again, that requires a change in political discourse and in the questions that are raised and answered.

First, is it likely that a reduction of control over Tier III countries by the United States would mean an increase of controls by the Soviet Union, China, or Cuba? It is not difficult to show that the entrance of the latter countries into the politics and policies of Tier III countries has, since World War II, almost invariably *followed* the entrance of the United States and U.S. attempts to shape and redirect the processes of change in the newly independent countries of Tier III.

Faced with U.S. might and intransigence, those who sought to break loose from foreign domination had to turn somewhere for help: Vietnam, to its ancient enemy China and the mistrusted Soviet Union; Cuba, under economic blockade (still in de jure if less in de facto force) and unable to sell to the United States its main (almost its only) export, sugar, looking also to the Soviet Union; Angola and Nicaragua, to Cuba and the Soviet Union; and so on. The Soviet Union has been neither idealistic nor innocent in its foreign activities, whether in or outside Europe, but if one seeks to establish causation for the turbulence in Tier III, it will be found in the attempts to maintain long-standing capitalist domination of Tier III, a process dominated by the United States since World War II. Here, as in the other proposals made earlier, it may be assumed that the process of change can come to justify itself. With a change in U.S. policies toward the Tier III countries, it may be assumed that acceptable changes by the adversary countries would become feasible.

But setting aside so-called strategic considerations, what of the political economy of softened—less exploitative and less draining—relationships with Tier III countries? The cheap labor and raw materials of Tier III are a tragedy for them.[29] Are they the boon they have seemed to be for Tiers I and II? Could the economies of the latter function well with lessened exploitation of Tier III? A major point of this book is that the enormous productive capacities of contemporary capitalism are such that the incomes of the leading countries cannot be maintained *unless* their own bottom income layers and those of the poor countries are lifted. Under contemporary conditions, if the world's low incomes do not rise toward the top, its high incomes will fall toward the bottom, the opposite of what has been generally believed.

The reality since World War II has been for the gap between the incomes of Tiers I and II and that of Tier III to widen, and this has been so in good times and bad. In the years up through the 1960s, the real incomes at the top and at the bottom were rising, the latter more slowly; in the years of crisis, incomes at the top have stabilized or fallen, and they have fallen even more rapidly at the bottom. The gap always widens. Whatever that process might have meant in the rosier days of the past (rosier at the top), its continuity now and for the future spells economic disaster for all. If nothing else, the increasingly unpayable debts of Tier III will crack the international financial system wide open.

Times have changed, and attitudes and institutions must change accordingly. The capitalism of the post–World War II era prospered in critical part because it found ways to *lessen* exploitation in the leading countries (as represented in rising real per capita consumption), as it spread and increased in Tier III. The labor exploitation of nineteenth-century Britain, Germany, and the United States (among others) was not different in kind from that of Tier III today—with respect to the mines, mills, or agriculture of the nineteenth century. There were few indeed who believed that capitalism could grow and flourish otherwise. Adam Smith, David Ricardo, and Karl Marx all agreed on at least one matter: Capital could not pay more than subsistence wages if profitability and capital accumulation were to occur. (And "subsistence" then meant what it now means in Tier III: a brief and terrible life.[30])

But what was so essential in the nineteenth century had, by the opening of the twentieth, lost its usefulness as such. The argument to that end could have been and was made before World War I, to no avail; it took at least half a century of misery and bloodshed to clear the institutional decks of the earlier capitalism and to begin to rebuild— with, of all things, consumerism having a prominent place in the new structure. The capitalists who had created the world of mass production well before World War I could only dimly see that mass production requires mass consumption and that the latter requires institutions substantially different from anything dreamed of by Adam Smith. What was true for the internal functioning of the leading capitalist nations before World War II (and temporarily remedied after World War II) is now applicable to Tier III: Its peoples must become something more than impoverished and oppressed hewers of wood and drawers of water. Just as now the workers of the Tier III countries increasingly work with the latest technologies, their countries must also see rising levels of real per capita consumption: of food, clothing, shelter, medical care, and education. Once more the capitalist world stands at a critical juncture: It must find ways to change its institutions so as to lessen human misery, or it will change so as to increase it greatly.

"Justice is a power," philosopher G. Lowes Dickinson once said, "and if it cannot create, it will destroy." It is expecting too much to hope for policies impelled by considerations of justice, but that is not intended here. Here, the argument runs in terms of mutual needs and possibilities, and of disasters, economic and military, as the alternative. Just before World War I, Thorstein Veblen (one of the best of U.S. social scientists, but widely neglected) could see the choices just then appearing over the horizon, and he wrote: "history records more frequent and more spectacular instances of the triumph of imbecile institutions over life and culture than of peoples who have by force of instinctive insight saved themselves alive out of a desperately precarious institutional situation, such, for instance, as now faces the people of Christendom."[31] The "imbecile institutions" triumphed once more, and the sluices of misery and blood ran wide open. This need not happen again, but it will, unless society changes its mind and its institutions. This can and must be done by combining two changes: the lessening of militarization and the lessening of exploitation, not as do-gooders or as peaceniks, but as peoples who wish to save themselves alive.

In the United States especially (but by no means only), this means that people must self-consciously come to grips with the realities of their daily existence, instead of allowing themselves to be lulled into catastrophe by nostalgic fantasies and infantile scenarios for the future, or to be terrorized by fears of "Reds" or "Arabs," or whoever. Understanding of the historical process and of society is difficult at any time, even under the best of circumstances, and then always incomplete, but it is quite impossible when the world is seen through the distorting lenses of a cold war, of nameless fears of the poor, let alone when all of these are mixed with the poison of racism. In such a world, the means for social understanding are deflected by the acceptance of double standards: What *we* do is OK (because our intentions and morality are of the highest); what *they* do is wrong, or dangerous (because *their* intentions and lack of morality are of the basest). If we have missiles in Turkey on the Soviet border, it is OK; if they have missiles in Cuba, "ninety miles from our shores," it is worth threatening world war to have them removed. Of course missiles shouldn't be at anyone's borders; but wherever they are, the intentions and the morality (or lack of it) are likely to be much the same for both sides. So it has been before, during, and after all wars. And what is true for military posturing and attitudes is not much different for points of view toward poor countries or poor people in rich countries. Moreover, racist attitudes depend upon that same ready access to the double standard.

Nations and people are of course different from each other, but their similarities in motivation, need, and ethical standards are more alike than diverse. Today, more than ever before in history, all societies and people are crowded into the same boat, heading in the same direction— a probable economic disaster and an increasingly likely nuclear war. The differences among and between all peoples will not be erased swiftly or, finally, at all, nor would it be desirable if they were. The similarities, in terms of need and possibility, must today push and pull the nations toward devising mutually beneficial solutions to their interdependent problems and their chronic crisis.

Whatever else that means, and some of it has been sketched above, it means that steps to increase the productivity, the incomes, the well-being, and the independence of Tier III countries must begin as soon as feasible. Many would say those steps began long ago. Some would mean by that the relationships between Tier III countries and the imperial powers developed in the nineteenth century (or even much earlier); most in the United States would mean the relationships developed since the 1950s, when the Tier III countries became the Partners in Progress of the United States. But those relationships have meant a terrible and continuing deterioration in the qualitative and quantitative aspects of life for almost all in the Tier III countries, except for that thin slice of people at the top who run governments and/or businesses that are clients of Tiers I and II.

What is needed instead cannot be spelled out in this brief space. But the main directions can be suggested: Continuing development programs must be designed and controlled *by* the Tier III countries and *for* them, in real, not rhetorical, terms. This means their financing must be free of control by transnational corporations or external authorities of any sort: In short, something of a world developmental fund must become a reality.

Ways to channel the bare necessities of life, not least of all, food, must be developed so as to eliminate hunger (among other such desperate needs) by means of the surplus production (as matters now stand) of the agricultural producers and, where relevant, of industrialists. Programs can and must be developed that utilize the latent skills and talents of the (mostly young) people of all tiers to provide the vital assistance needed in the realms of health and education (and also important, though less dramatic, transportation and engineering): a mammoth and "disinterested peace corps," or some such, which, like the U.S. Peace Corps, would be most inviting to young people, especially if it were genuinely disinterested. One could go on. But in addition to the financial proposals made earlier, a critical change that must be made is that which encourages and allows more representative, more democratic, govern- ments to take hold in Tier III. In turn that means the beginning of the end of the military dictatorships that are so common and that so often get and stay in power because of foreign support and arms. The rotten and cruel governments that exist in Tier III are not wanted by the peoples of those countries; they have been seen as needed (as a "lesser evil") by the major powers. The whole world pays and may yet pay considerably more. Enough already.

Enough of such laundry lists of social change. The problem is not to concoct but to work for changes. It is possible as well as desirable and necessary to do that work. With will and imagination and a little instinctive insight—with even a tentative extension of the normal social decency people have been taught to distrust—who knows? Society might be able to pass through this crisis into a world of more hope and less fear, even, perhaps into a world of less hate and more love. The alternatives to trying are pretty grim.

Notes

1. In the United States, the utilization of capacity in manufacturing has risen significantly as a consequence of the long and large fall in the dollar, and exports and profits have risen, but the annual trade deficit has stayed above the $150 billion level. What is good for U.S. manufacturing is not so good for world manufacturing, however, as noted earlier.

2. See R. T. Naylor, *Hot Money and the Politics of Debt* (New York: Linden Press/Simon and Schuster, 1987), pp. 11–30. An economics professor at McGill University (Canada), Naylor has an unusually broad perspective that has allowed him to treat all the major connections in the financial world, including vital ones with the underworld.

3. Antonio Gramsci was leader of the Italian Communist party when Mussolini took power. He was imprisoned for over a decade and died as a result. A manifestation of his "optimism of the will" was his important writing done in prison. See, e.g., Quintin Hoare and G. N. Smith (eds.), *Selections from the Prison Notebooks of Antonio Gramsci* (London: Lawrence and Wishart, 1971).

4. See Naylor, *Hot Money*, Pt. 2.

5. Howard Wachtel, *The Money Mandarins* (New York: Pantheon, 1986), p. 397. His "Third World" is roughly my Tier III. The debt of 1984, noted by him, was small as compared to today's.

6. Naylor, *Hot Money*, pp. 36–37. See also his entire Chap. 2, "Eurodollars and Nonsense," pp. 31–46.

7. Susan Strange, *Casino Capitalism* (Oxford: Basil Blackwell, 1986), pp. 176–177.

8. Ibid.

9. See Felix Rohatyn, "On the Brink," *New York Review of Books*, June 11, 1987. Citibank was soon followed by other banks that have been also heavily involved.

10. Naylor, *Hot Money*, p. 16 (his emphasis). A comprehensive critique of the origins and nature of the debt of Tier III, and a detailed program for reform is put forth in Peter Körner, Gero Maass, Thomas Siebold, and Rainer Tetzlaff, *The IMF and the Debt Crisis: A Guide to the Third World's Dilemma* (London: Zed Books, Ltd., 1986), especially Chapters 4 and 5. The authors saw IMF stabilization policies as cures likely to kill the patient and called for deep structural reforms requiring the powerful countries and the weaker ones to solve the debt problem by moving toward the resolution of the larger problems of badly needed economic development—but of a different type than that pushed up to now by the creditor countries. A useful guide to the long-term and recent development of international banking, including the financial fever that led to, among other problems, the dangerous indebtedness of the poorer countries, is Anthony Sampson, *The Money Lenders: Bankers and a World In Turmoil* (New York: Viking Press, 1982), and Martin Mayer, *The Fate of the Dollar* (New York: Truman Talley Books/Times Books, 1980).

11. Also among the losers are those who depend upon industrial or agricultural exports to Tier III countries. Those exports have declined dramatically in the 1980s, about 30–40 percent from the United States to Latin America, alone. This has not directly harmed the giant creditor banks in the United States; indirectly it has, as seen in the collapse of Continental Illinois (with its many agricultural and oil loans). More important are the industrial jobs that have been lost.

12. See Naylor, *Hot Money*, pp. 368–370.

13. See the strong analysis of Arthur MacEwan in Richard Edwards et al., *The Capitalist System* (Englewood Cliffs, N.J.: Prentice-Hall, 1986), pp. 107–117. For Tier III military expenditures, see Saadet Deger, *Military Expenditures in Third World Countries* (London: Routledge and Kegan Paul, 1986). Since the 1960s those expenditures have risen much more rapidly than military expenditures in the United States or the Soviet Union. The United States is not the only culprit in this tragedy, of course: the Soviet Union's exploits in Afghanistan and Ethiopia come to mind. But in any contest about the militarization of Tier III countries, the United States would be the clear winner.

14. See Deger, *Military Expenditures*, and R. L. Sivard, *World Military and Social Expenditures* (Washington, D.C.: World Priorities, 1983), for the patterns of military expenditures and Sivard for social expenditures as well.

15. Mikhail Gorbachev's *Perestroika* (New York: Harper & Row, 1987) is striking both in its reasoning and its proposals; and also encouraging. For population estimates and casualties, see Gregory Frumkin, *Population Changes in Europe Since 1939* (New York: McGraw-Hill, 1951). Writing as a population specialist for the United Nations, he put Soviet losses at 28 million, civilian plus military.

16. Jerry W. Sanders, "Security and Choice," in *World Policy Journal* 1, no. 4, p. 721 (Summer 1984). Sanders made strong political and economic arguments that harmonize well with my own proposals.

17. Lester C. Thurow, *The Zero-Sum Society: Distribution and the Possibilities for Economic Change* (New York: Basic Books, 1980), p. 10. As defined on p. 11, "a zero-sum game is any game where the losses exactly equal the winnings. All sporting events are zero-sum games." Although evidently not true of Thurow, all too many economists do in fact think of economics as some kind of game, for their own pleasure and gain.

18. With very few, honorable, and marginalized exceptions, the economics profession throughout this increasingly and broadly wasteful century, although it sees itself as being concerned squarely with "the allocation of *scarce* resources to unlimited wants," has not taken the occasion to acknowledge, let alone to analyze and study what is here termed "the political economy of destruction and waste." There are many damning criticisms to make of this and the other social "sciences," but this failing must surely rank near the top in a world where so many are desperately poor.

19. Alan Wolfe, *America's Impasse: The Rise and Fall of the Politics of Growth* (Boston: South End Press, 1981), pp. 250–253. Among the many books proposing changes of this general nature for the United States are Samuel Bowles et al., *Beyond the Waste Land: A Democratic Alternative to Economic Decline* (New York: Anchor Doubleday, 1983), Ronald E. Muller, *Revitalizing America* (New York: Simon and Schuster, 1980), Gar Alperovitz and Jeff Faux, *Rebuilding America* (New York: Simon and Schuster, 1981), Barry Bluestone and Bennett Harrison, *The Deindustrialization of America* (New York: Basic Books, 1982), and Martin Carnoy and Derek Shearer, *Economic Democracy: The Challenge of the 1980s* (New York: Sharpe, 1980). Walter Russell Mead, in his *Mortal Splendor: The American Empire in Transition* (Boston: Houghton Mifflin, 1987), puts forth a general framework for change in both domestic and foreign policies compatible with what I have offered in these pages. See his Part 6. It is a symptom of a certain hopefulness, as well as of the deepening crisis, that a new set of proposals for change emerges almost monthly; moreover, they tend to overlap.

20. The data concerning inadequate housing, rising homelessness, educational decline, and poverty are troubling to the point of scandal in the United States. Even more scandalous are the data for health care, which effectively represents much else in "the quality of life." About $500 billion annually is spent in the United States on health care, about 11 percent of GNP; yet it is generally recognized that both the quantitative and the qualitative availability of health care is substantially less adequate for ordinary people in the United States than it is elsewhere in the industrialized world—where the costs are lower, per capita.

An ugly and representative category of this condition was provided in a news release from the U.S. Congressional Office of Technology Assessment: "More than 40,000 American babies die annually before their first birthdays, about 1 percent of all babies born. In 1985, the U.S. infant mortality rate—10.6 deaths per 1,000 infants—ranked 17th internationally. . . . Between 1978 and 1984, although the proportion of American infants living in poverty rose from 18 to 24 percent, Medicaid expenditures per child declined by 13 percent and federal funds of major health programs for poor women and children decreased by 32 percent." The report went on to say that an expansion of the Medicaid program to cover all pregnant women with incomes below the federal poverty level would cost only $4 million annually—and would save about twice that amount in hospital costs associated with low-birthweight infants. See *Washington Post*, March 10, 1988. For discussions of housing, health, and associated matters, see Chapters 3 ("Valuation of Human Life and Health"), 6 ("Old Age"), and 9 ("Slums and Poverty"), in John E. Ullman (ed.), *Social Costs in Modern Society* (Westport, Conn.: Quorum Books, 1983). For a broad and penetrating analysis, see James O'Connor, *Accumulation Crisis* (New York: Blackwell's, 1984), Chapter 6, "The Process of Consumption," wherein the author connected these and other deplorable failings to the intrinsic characteristics of the socioeconomic system. The Reagan administration has rightly received much criticism for the ways in which it has cut away at the social "safety net." But it must be noted that the "net" has never been more than flimsy and that its inadequacies are systemic.

21. *International Herald Tribune*, December 21, 1986. In the same issue was a long analysis of restrictive agricultural policies in the nations of the European Economic Community (EC) whose headline read: "Mounting Food Surpluses Threaten to Push EC Into Bankruptcy." For searching analyses of the whys and wherefores of the cruelty and consequences (and high profits for a few) of the global food problem, see Jon Bennett, *The Hunger Machine: The Politics of Food* (New York: B. Blackwell, 1987), and not least the introduction by Susan George. The latter has for many years been the most astute, informed, and enraged of those who study this area. See her *How the Other Half Dies: The Real Reasons for World Hunger* (Totowa, N.J.: Rowman, 1977), *Feeding the Few: Corporate Control of Food* (Washington, D.C.: Institute for Policy Studies, 1979), and *Ill Fares the Land: Essays on Food, Hunger, and Power* (Washington, D.C.: Institute for Policy Studies, 1984).

22. See Nick Kotz, *Wild Blue Yonder: Money, Politics, and the B-1 Bomber* (New York: Pantheon, 1987), a study that revealed many of the dimensions of what is wrong with military spending.

23. Emma Rothschild, "Reagan and the Real America," *New York Review of Books*, February 6, 1981. For considerably more detail, see Bluestone and Harrison, *Deindustrialization of America*. The years since 1981 have been described and analyzed in a penetrating two-part essay by Emma Rothschild: "The Real Reagan Economy" and "The Reagan Economic Legacy," in *New York Review of Books*, June 30 and July 21, 1988, respectively.

24. For what is wrong with the welfare system in the United States, for its benefactors and its beneficiaries (both reluctant), see F. Piven and R. Cloward,

Regulating the Poor: The Functions of Public Welfare (New York: Vintage, 1971); and for the recent savaging of even that already weak system, see the same authors' *The New Class War: Reagan's Attack on the Welfare State and Its Consequences* (New York: Pantheon, 1982). Sol Yurick's *The Bag*, a novel about that system in New York City during the 1960s, is a vivid portrait of the degradation of all involved. That the system works in these ways is a consequence of the manner in which the poor, the unemployed, the disabled, et al., are viewed within the framework of capitalist ideology. See William Ryan, *Blaming the Victim* (New York: Random House, 1972).

25. Jonathan Kozol, when he was a high school teacher in Boston in the 1960s, began to uncover the elements of the educational tragedy in his *Death at an Early Age: The Destruction of the Hearts and Minds of Negro School Children in the Boston Public Schools* (Boston: Houghton Mifflin, 1967). More recently, he has enlarged his scope in *Illiterate America* (Garden City, N.Y.: Anchor Press/ Doubleday, 1985). An alternative path, valuing both children and education, is described in the eloquent book by George Dennison, *The Lives of Children* (New York: Random House, 1969). The Reagan era has provoked many critiques, of course. Among the most useful of them are Robert Lekachman, *Greed is Not Enough: Reaganomics* (New York: Pantheon, 1982), and the excellent collection of essays edited by Colin Greer and Frank Riessman, *What Reagan Is Doing to Us* (New York: Harper & Row, 1982).

26. The interview was with Richard Reeves, "Whatever It Is, It Still Makes Sammy Run," published in *International Herald Tribune*, August 19, 1987.

27. R. H. Tawney, *The Acquisitive Society* (New York: Harcourt, Brace, 1920), p. 180. The quotation about greed, from a nineteenth-century economist, is found on p. 27.

28. Gabriel Kolko, *Main Currents in American History* (New York: Pantheon, 1984), Chapters 10 and 11.

29. There are a few real and a few apparent exceptions. Singapore has probably seen a generally rising level of life for the majority of its (very small) population. An apparent but not real exception is South Korea; something in between is Taiwan.

30. There is of course an enormous literature on nineteenth-century capitalist development. For a discussion of the main point of this paragraph, see G.D.H. Cole and Raymond Postgate, *The British Common People, 1746–1946* (London: Methuen, 1961).

31. Thorstein Veblen, *The Instinct of Workmanship* (New York: B. W. Huebsch, 1914), p. 125. Veblen's strictures against waste and what he saw as the basic irrationality of capitalism, ran through all his many books. I have attempted to present a coherent view of his entire work in my *Thorstein Veblen* (New York: Washington Square Press, 1964).

Suggestions for Further Reading

Chapter 1

The term *crisis* is used often but not always used well. For an analytical survey of the term and its current dimensions, see James O'Connor, *The Meaning of Crisis* (New York: Basil Blackwell, 1987). The sweep of the entire post–World War II period was ably captured in Herman Van der Wee, *Prosperity and Upheaval, 1945–1980* (New York: Viking Penguin, 1986). The long-run trends producing current realities were early and well analyzed in Josef Steindl, *Maturity and Stagnation in American Capitalism* (New York: Monthly Review Press, 1976; first published, 1952). The possibilities of financial breakdown have for many years preoccupied Professor Hyman P. Minsky. See his *Can It Happen Again? Essays in Instability and Finance* (Armonk, N.Y.: M. E. Sharpe, 1982).

Mainstream social understanding suffers from weaknesses derived from its ways of reasoning, its "methodology." For useful approaches to this, see C. Wright Mills, *The Sociological Imagination* (New York: Oxford University Press, 1967), Joan Robinson, *Economic Philosophy* (Chicago: Aldine, 1962), Benjamin Ward, *What's Wrong with Economics* (New York: Basic Books, 1972), and E. K. Hunt and Jesse Schwartz (eds.), *A Critique of Economic Theory* (Harmondsworth, U.K.: Penguin, 1972). A critical approach by historians is found in William Appleman Williams, *The Great Evasion* (Chicago: Quadrangle, 1964), and in his influential and powerful *Contours of American History* (Cleveland: World Publishing, 1961), as well as in Howard Zinn, *A People's History of the United States* (New York: Harper & Row, 1980). Those who wish to start from scratch in economics will find the following introductory text useful for both critical and conventional analysis and even entertaining: Tom Riddell et al., *Economics: A Tool for Social Understanding* (Reading, Mass.: Addison Wesley, 1987).

The influence of the United States on the Japanese economy after 1945 (alluded to in the text) is treated usefully in John Toland, *Occupation* (New York: Doubleday, 1987), and in Theodore Cohen, *Remaking Japan: The American Occupation as New Deal* (Glencoe, Ill.: The Free Press, 1987). Gorbachev's proposals for the Soviet Union are analyzed and viewed critically (but not hostilely) by Soviet scholar Marshall Goldman, in *Gorbachev's Challenge* (New York: W. W. Norton, 1987).

The problem of hunger in the world is usually treated as a problem of geography and resources, as a physical problem. That such is not the case is shown clearly and profoundly in the classic of Josué de Castro (a Brazilian scientist), in his *The Geopolitics of Hunger* (New York: Monthly Review Press, 1977; first published, 1952, as *The Geography of Hunger*).

Chapter 2

Thorstein Veblen was probably the first to foresee the probabilities and consequences of modern industrial capitalism, as put forth in his *Theory of Business Enterprise* (New York: Scribner, 1904), and *Absentee Ownership and Business Enterprise in Recent Times* (New York: B. W. Huebsch, 1923; Viking, 1954). In those books, Veblen focused on the United States. Robert A. Brady, who was much influenced by Veblen (and also by Marx), was able years later to study the same tendencies in all the leading capitalist countries, in his *Business as a System of Power* (New York: Columbia University Press, 1943), individually and as a system. The passage of many decades has not reduced the power of either Veblen's or Brady's analyses.

Contemporary thinking is well represented in Samuel Bowles and Richard Edwards, *Understanding Capitalism: Competition, Command, and Change in the U.S. Economy* (New York: Harper & Row, 1985), and in Samuel Bowles and Herbert Gintis, *Democracy and Capitalism: Property, Community, and the Contradictions of Modern Social Thought* (New York: Basic Books, 1987). Detailed studies of economic organization are found in Walter Adams and James W. Brock, *The Bigness Complex: Industry, Labor, and Government in the American Economy* (New York: Pantheon, 1986), and on a more popular level, Morton Mintz and Jerry S. Cohen, *America, Inc.* (New York: Dell, 1971).

The social and political structures that interact with the economy are strikingly analyzed in C. Wright Mills, *The Power Elite* (New York: Oxford University Press, 1956). Much influenced by Mills is G. William Domhoff, *The Higher Circles* (New York: Vintage, 1971). See also Maurice Zeitlin, *American Society, Inc.* (Chicago: Markham, 1970), and Ira Katznelson and Mark Kesselman, *The Politics of Power* (New York: Harcourt Brace Jovanovich, 1975).

The overlapping powers of the giant corporations and the giant state are discussed and analyzed in James O'Connor, *The Corporations and the State* (New York: Harper & Row, 1974), which includes an excellent essay on economic imperialism. Central to that phenomenon in today's world is the multinational corporation. Its origins and implications were early (perhaps first) understood by the late Stephen Hymer. See his *The Multinational Corporation: A Radical Approach* (Cambridge: Cambridge University Press, 1979).

The crosscurrents of contemporary capitalism are many and confusing. An aid to understanding may be found in two books by Professor Edward Nell: *Free Market Conservatism: A Critique of Theory and Practice* and *Transformational*

Growth and the Role of Government (Winchester, Mass.: Allen & Unwin, 1984 and 1988, respectively). Also broadly helpful is Alan Wolfe, *The Limits of Legitimacy: Political Contradictions of Advanced Capitalism* (New York: Free Press, 1980). The complexities of post–World War II development outside the United States are well described and analyzed in Andrew Shonfield, *Modern Capitalism: The Changing Balance of Public and Private Power* (New York: Oxford University Press, 1969). Stephen Ambrose, *Rise to Globalism* (New York: Penguin, 1985), traced the path of the United States through the decades since 1945.

As emphasized in the text, monopoly capitalism is not only economics and politics; it is also psychology and sociology, for it requires what Gramsci called "the consenting acceptance" of the ordinary people if it is to work smoothly and to persist. There is a large and growing literature regarding the phenomena of conformity and mind management. Among the most useful books are Jerry Mander, *Four Arguments for the Elimination of Television* (New York: Morrow, 1978), and Rose K. Goldsen, *The Show and Tell Machine* (New York: Dial Press, 1977), regarding TV. For the press, see Robert Cirino, *Don't Blame the People* (New York: Random House, 1971), and James Aronson, *The Press and the Cold War* (Indianapolis: Bobbs-Merrill, 1970). Stuart Ewen plumbed a major dimension of modern life in his *Advertising and the Social Roots of the Consumer Culture* (New York: McGraw-Hill, 1976), and Russell Jacoby probed even more deeply in his attempt to understand conformism as it affects not only the public but the psychological/psychiatric professionals, in his *Social Amnesia* (Boston: Beacon Press, 1975).

The cold war has been inextricably commingled in the economic, political, military, and sociocultural history of the last several decades. In its absence, the lives of all the peoples in the world would have been altered beyond compare with what has instead occurred: It has been "the fix" of many people's lives, especially those in the United States. Much has been written on its origins and meanings, of course. Fundamental among the studies is that of D. F. Fleming, *The Cold War and Its Origins: 1917–1960*, 2 vols. (Garden City, N.Y.: Doubleday, 1961). Covering roughly the same years, in a most readable and penetrating analysis, is Carl Oglesby and Richard Shaull, *Containment and Change* (New York: Macmillan, 1967), Part 1. An excellent (and neglected) history of the post–World War II period is Lawrence Wittner, *Cold War America* (New York: Harper & Row, 1978). The Indochina war was among the worst products of the cold war. A fine book for assistance in comprehending that badly understood catastrophe is William Appleman Williams, *America in Vietnam: A Documentary History* (Garden City, N.Y.: Anchor, 1985). But also see Frances Fitzgerald, *Fire in the Lake* (Boston: Atlantic Monthly Press, 1972), and Richard Barnet, *Intervention and Revolution* (New York: World Publishing, 1968).

Chapter 3

Supplementing the basic works on the world economy cited in the text are the more specialized and detailed studies of Alfred Maizels, *Industrial Growth and World Trade: An Empirical Study of Trends in Production, Consumption and*

Trade in Manufactures from 1899–1959 (Cambridge: Cambridge University Press, 1965), and two studies by Folke Hilgerdt, *The Network of World Trade* and *Industrialization and Foreign Trade* (Geneva: League of Nations, 1942 and 1946, respectively). Also very useful for both data and analysis is Ingvar Svennilson, *Growth and Stagnation in Europe* (Geneva: United Nations, 1954), with data connecting and comparing the periods before World War I and before World War II and a provocative analysis of the weaknesses of the interwar period, which Svennilson saw as "stagnation." More briefly, and with an analysis that ties the troubles of the leading and lesser countries together, with useful information on each of the leading countries' economic processes, is W. Arthur Lewis, *Economic Survey, 1919–1939* (London: Allen & Unwin, 1949).

Paul Baran, in his *Political Economy of Growth* (New York: Monthly Review Press, 1957) also made the connections between the two worlds of economic strength and weakness but did so through the framework of imperialism. That work was highly influential for many analysts in the years since, not least of them André Gunder Frank, influential in his own right with his "dependency analysis." See his *Dependent Accumulation and Underdevelopment* (New York: Monthly Review Press, 1979). Overlapping is Michael Tanzer's *The Race for Resources: Continuing Struggles Over Minerals and Fuels* (New York: Monthly Review Press, 1980). Also useful is Donald W. Attwood, Thomas C. Bruneau, and John G. Galaty (eds.), *Power and Poverty: Development and Development Projects in the Third World* (Boulder, Colo.: Westview Press, 1987).

The years since 1945 have witnessed an unprecedented intertwining of economic, political, and military processes and of the private and the governmental: grants, loans, aid, investment, some benign, most not. The literature on all this is enormous. Among the more useful studies are H. B. Price, *The Marshall Plan and Its Meanings* (Ithaca: Cornell University Press, 1955). Considerably more critical, and concerned with the Third World, are Teresa Hayter and Cathy Watson, *Aid: Rhetoric and Reality* (London: Pluto Press, 1985), dealing with British policies; and Cheryl Payer, *The Debt Trap: The IMF and the Third World* and *The World Bank: A Critical Analysis* (New York: Monthly Review Press, 1975 and 1982, respectively).

The shakiness of both U.S. and global finance is the subject of an increasing number of books, including Adrian Hamilton, *The Financial Revolution* (Glencoe, Ill.: Free Press, 1986), Irving H. Sprague, *Bailout: An Insider's Account of Bank Failures and Rescues* (New York: Basic Books, 1986), and Benjamin J. Cohen, *In Whose Interest? International Banking and American Foreign Policy* (New Haven: Yale University Press, 1986).

U.S. foreign policy, whether in regard to the major powers or the Third World, is almost universally seen as aimed at the betterment of all by the citizens of the United States, even though it is also consistent with the self-interest (economic or strategic) of the United States and even if the foreign policy sometimes mysteriously backfires. A sharply different understanding has been put forth in a variety of books. Among them are Joyce and Gabriel Kolko, *The Limits of Power: The World and United States Foreign Policy, 1945–1954* (New York: Harper & Row, 1972), Walter LaFeber, *America, Russia, and the Cold War* (New York:

John Wiley and Sons, 1967), and the same author's *Inevitable Revolutions* (New York: W. W. Norton, 1984), concerned with Central America. Also important is James F. Petras et al., *Latin America: Bankers, Generals, and the Struggle for Social Justice* (Totowa, N.J.: Rowman and Allanheld, 1986). Noam Chomsky has long been a strenuous critic of U.S. foreign policy. Among his most damning critiques is *American Power and the New Mandarins* (New York: Vintage, 1969) and, much later, with Edward S. Herman, *The Washington Connection and Third World Fascism* (Boston: South End Press, 1979).

Departing from an entirely different perspective, but increasingly troubled by the disintegration of the world created so swiftly and easily by the United States after 1945, is the thoughtful examination of David P. Calleo, *Beyond American Hegemony: The Future of the Western Alliance* (New York: Basic Books, 1987). Writing from a considerably more critical standpoint is Joyce Kolko, in her *Restructuring the World Economy* (New York: Pantheon Books, 1988). She covered the entire post–World War II period in some ways, but her emphasis is on the period 1974–1980. The wealth of her data and the power of her analysis combine to make this the most compelling study of the recent past and a warning of what lies ahead.

Chapter 4

A main aim of this book has been to reveal the strong connecting links of the long chain of what are misleadingly called "problems": between war and waste and overcapacity and hunger and environmental damage and greed and power and war and waste and so on. Barry Commoner, an eminent biologist, has in a different but compatible way sought to do the same. In his *The Poverty of Power: Energy and the Economic Crisis* (New York: Knopf, 1976), he showed clearly that there is no need for either a food or an energy shortage, among many other matters. E. J. Mishan, in *Technology and Growth: The Price We Pay* (New York: Praeger, 1969), argued convincingly that the heavy reliance of the United States upon mindless economic growth cannot but have devastating effects upon the quality of people's lives; and that such a reliance is as stupid as it is unnecessary. Barry Weisberg, in his *Beyond Repair: The Ecology of Capitalism* (Boston: Beacon Press, 1971), saw these same matters as produced by an irrational system, rather than by stupidity. Bringing the two positions together in some sense is James Ridgeway's *The Politics of Ecology* (New York: Dutton, 1971). Robert L. Heilbroner, in *The Human Prospect* (New York: W. W. Norton, 1974), has put forth a careful, clear, and deeply gloomy analysis of past, present, and future that one can only hope is wrong.

It would be difficult to overestimate the damage done to urban existence in this century by the "automobilization" of economy and society—among other damages, not least to the air. What cities have been, can be, and, in an important sense, must be is treated in a manner both scholarly and moving by Lewis Mumford in *The City and History* (New York: Harcourt Brace Jovanovich, 1961). How the automobile has ravaged the city is analyzed in his *The Highway and the City* (New York: Harcourt Brace Jovanovich, 1958). The flight from city to suburbs has been both disruptive and disturbing in its consequences and social implications, as seen by Richard Sennett, *The Uses of Disorder* (New York: Random House, 1970).

And then, constituting much of the dirty work of the wasteful and destructive world are the military and the CIA. The literature, most of its critical, is justly vast in this area. Among the best works are Herbert I. Schiller and Joseph D. Phillips, *Super-State: Readings in the Military-Industrial Complex* (Urbana, Ill.: University of Illinois Press, 1972), Michael T. Klare, *American Arms Supermarket* (Austin: University of Texas Press, 1985), and, with Cynthia Aronson, *Supplying Repression: U.S. Support for Authoritarian Regimes Abroad* (Washington, D.C.: Institute for Policy Studies, 1984). On the CIA and covert activities, both sinister and bumbling, see *Secret Warriors: Inside the Covert Military Operations of the Reagan Era* (New York: G. P. Putnam's Sons, 1988), by Steven Emerson. Stretching further back in time are John Prados, *Presidents' Secret Wars: CIA and Pentagon Covert Operations Since World War II* (New York: Morrow, 1986), and Morton Halperin, Jerry Berman, Robert Borosage, and Christine Marwick, *The Lawless State* (New York: Penguin, 1978). And I remind the reader of the references made to the works of Melman, Cypher, and Landau in the text.

Chapter 5

As are all other countries in the world, the United States is marked by deep inequalities in its distributions of income, wealth, power, and opportunity. Inequalities cannot be erased within the capitalist framework, but they can be, and at times have been, lessened by economic and social policies, through tax and expenditure policies. Much more has been done along such lines in Western Europe than in the United States, especially in regard to minimum levels of income and access to decent housing and health care. Even more shocking is the great and growing gap between the living conditions of the people of the Third World and those of the powerful societies. A major theme of this book has been that only by a positive reduction of that gap between poor and well-off, within and between countries, can the well-being of the rich countries be maintained. The additional readings that follow put forth arguments and proposals that are congruent with that goal, though not usually stated in exactly the same ways as mine.

To begin with, there is an important group of essays by R. H. Tawney, *Equality* (New York: Capricorn Books, 1961; originally published, 1931). Tawney was one of the seminal social thinkers of this century, appalled by the sense-lessness, the cruelty, and the dangers of the leading U.S. institutions. How those institutions have adversely affected the lives of sizable portions of the U.S. population was analyzed in different ways by Bradley Schiller, *Poverty and Discrimination* (Englewood Cliffs, N.J.: Prentice-Hall, 1981), Michael Reich, *Racial Inequality: A Political-Economic Analysis* (Princeton: Princeton University Press, 1981), and Howard Wachtel, *Labor and the Economy* (New York: Academic Press, 1984), all of whom provide important data and analyses. The structures and processes discussed in those books are not intractable but deep-seated and damaging to the entire society, as is shown by Ben Seligman, *Permanent Poverty: An American Syndrome* (New York: Quadrangle, 1968).

To change the ugly patterns that increasingly dominate our lives in the United States, we must "disenthrall ourselves" of a great deal, not least of which is our attachment as a people to being "Number One." It would assist that effort at disenthrallment to read William Appleman Williams, *Empire as a Way of Life: An Essay on the Causes and Character of America's Present Predicament* (New York: Oxford University Press, 1980). It is also important to understand the background and meaning of the matters discussed by Fred Block et al., *The Mean Season: The Attack on the Welfare State* (New York: Pantheon, 1987).

Positive and particular proposals may be found in Marcus Raskin, *The Common Good: Its Politics, Policies, and Philosophy* (New York: Routledge and Kegan Paul, 1986), and in his book edited together with Chester Hartman, *Winning America: Ideas and Leadership for the 1990s* (Boston: South End Press, 1988), which proposes changes ranging from family policy and health care to military and foreign policy. Chester Hartman has long been involved as a city planner and a critic of city planning. His *Transformation of San Francisco* (Totowa, N.J.: Rowman and Allanheld, 1984) is an analysis of what has gone wrong and why and a positive approach that has meaning for a large number of cities in the United States. See also his *America's Housing Crisis: What Is to Be Done?* (London: Methuen, Inc., 1983).

Although most people in the United States are unaware of it, the availability and the quality of health care for the majority in this country is scandalously below that of all other industrial capitalist societies. Much of the reason why is explored well in Barbara and John Ehrenreich, *The American Health Empire* (New York: Random House, 1971). That it need not be so is made clear in Rashi Fein, *Medical Care, Medical Costs* (Cambridge: Harvard University Press, 1986).

I close with two books. The first puts forth a broad set of proposals that, if implemented only halfway, would do much to position the United States to overcome what is otherwise likely to draw us and the rest of the world to a wholly unnecessary tragedy: Martin Carnoy, Derek Shearer, and Russell Rumberger, *A New Social Contract: The Economy and Government After Reagan* (New York: Harper & Row, 1983). The other is a small and beautiful book by E. F. Schumacher, *Small Is Beautiful* (New York: Perennial Press, 1974). What the book proposes is suggested by its title. That Schumacher's hopes are vain for this hyped-up world is clear, and that was probably clear to him as well. But it is a stirring antidote to the modern affliction that presumes that bigger is better and biggest is best.

Periodicals

The search for social understanding implies endless reading; even as that is done, the goal remains elusive, an always-receding horizon. The reading must comprise old and new books, and it must include the study of daily, weekly, and monthly periodicals. Particularly useful mainstream journals that routinely discuss issues of importance are *Business Week*, the *Wall Street Journal*, the *Economist* (London), *Nation*, the *New York Review of Books*, and *World Policy Journal*. Critical periodicals that I recommend are *Monthly Review, In These Times*, and *Dollars and Sense*.

Index